THE POWER OF POWERLESSNESS

ROBIN OAKE

WITH SHEILA JACOBS

10 Publishing
a division of 10 of those.com

First published in Great Britain in 2015

British Library Cataloguing in Publication Data
A record for this book is available from the British Library

ISBN: 978-1-910587-08-9

Designed & typeset by Pete Barnsley (Creative Hoot)
Cover image copyright: mikeexpert / 123RF Stock Photo
Printed in the UK by CPI

10Publishing, a division of 10ofthose.com
9D Centurion Court, Farington, Leyland, PR25 3UQ, England

Email: info@10ofthose.com
Website: www.10ofthose.com

CONTENTS

Preface

1 How real is this Christianity?

2 Forgive others – even God?

3 I can't overcome my sins

4 I feel so stressed

5 Bullying, ostracism and not being part of the crowd

6 Surely there's no hope for the criminal?

7 Imprisoned and persecuted for faith

8 Families, friends and neighbours

9 In sickness and in health

10 When darkness falls

11 Life is not trouble free

12 This is the crunch

PREFACE

'Stop thief!' 'Hey, come back ...' 'Oi, stop ...' 'Copper, chase him, he's just nicked a bundle of money from the counter ...!'

I had been standing at a busy junction watching the traffic and had my back to the noise and hullabaloo. Some 100 yards away I saw a figure running from view and the cry of a dozen or so men. It was the women who were shouting at him and me!

I was standing with an older colleague, who quickly said, 'After him, Robin. You're fit. He can't get anywhere running that way. He will arrive back with me if you chase hard.'

I heard the last bit and relished the run. Helmet in hand, I soon caught up with and went through the chasing group, and gradually gained on the track-suited man. He was evidently quite fit too, but eventually, as I got near, I shouted harshly and loudly, 'Stop. The game's up!'

He ran into the courtyard of an estate agent and then behind the building, where he leant against the fence as I caught his collar. There was no real struggle and, I think with my size and the police uniform, he just gave up. Phew! I was panting hard – probably more than he was – and had to catch my breath, but was about to start the caution when he dropped a bundle of £10 notes which he had in his left hand. Before I could issue the official caution he just went limp and said, 'I'm so sorry. I don't know what came over me.'

I was able to breathe out a question, 'Where did you get that money? Did you steal it?'

He could only look at the ground and then at a small crowd which had gathered to watch. He then mumbled, 'I was at the tube station and saw this bundle of notes by the window. Spur of the moment, without thinking, I snatched it.'

I simply said, 'I am arresting you for stealing the bundle' and cautioned him. I picked up the notes and took hold of his arm, and then marched him back through the crowd to the nearby police station.

My sergeant, with whom I played rugby, wasn't that pleased to see us arrive as he was about to go off duty, but when I related the facts of the theft and the chase, he whispered to me, 'Well done, Robin. We'll make a copper of you yet!'

The young man was charged and later released on bail. However, when I put him in a cell while his lodgings were verified and the paperwork done, I asked him what made him do it. He said, 'I am an athlete, an international one, but have a recurrent injury for which I take pain killers. I can't do without the drug now yet the dealer is costing me too much and I have little money.'

This was not an isolated incident either in my early career or with life in general. Picture a fit young man with a good reputation and well known for his athletic ability. As often happens with any athlete, usually at very inconvenient times before a championship or high-profile meeting, an injury occurs and doesn't immediately heal. Suddenly, as with this young man, the expectation of doing well at the next athletics meeting has evaporated. The physiotherapist tries hard to massage the injury, the medical staff do their best, but nothing is helping ... except the pain killers. The drugs are only effective for a short while as their potency diminishes, but the bills pile up, the dealer is angry ... and the once honoured and lauded athlete is now powerless. He has lost his agility – even a young copper in full uniform can catch up with him. He ends up in court and with a prison sentence. No longer selected for his team, he experiences a dreadful spiral of defeat, depression and disaster. What's left? The power of fitness, the elation of winning races and the adulation of the packed grandstands have all gone.

I use this illustration of many I could recall to help us all realise that there are times when we feel so low that we are helpless and hopeless. We are powerless to do anything about it. This book typifies the many in this world who come to the end of their tether – who have failed either because of their own ill-judgment or through circumstances beyond their control. Gradually or suddenly they are feeling worthless and powerless so either give up completely or,like this athlete, do something foolish in an effort to pull themselves up by their bootstraps.

I am illustrating failure but not defeat, and bring into perspective many who have fallen off the ladder of life but in their despondence have found, one way or another, that powerlessness is not the end. Even in the darkness of a black tunnel, there is a bend which reveals the light and ultimately a new power in their lives.

The pages of this book are, of course, for everyone to read, but are primarily aimed at two groups of people – those who are feeling lonely and down at the heel, and others who want to help them.

The Power of Powerlessness might seem a strange title for a book, but when one is powerless, the only way is up ... in a new power, with a new start and then with a testimony to help others who are where the powerless once was.

I draw on many years in the police service, in all ranks, to illustrate the excitement that there is when life is renewed. I have had to camouflage some of the instances to ensure that no one is embarrassed, but from some I have had the encouragement of the words: 'Use my story if it will help others in a similar predicament.'

I was prompted to write this short book by the words of the Apostle Paul who said, 'For when I am weak, then I am strong.' This would seem to be complete nonsense and quite illogical but the context gives the true substance of the assertion. You can read of this in Paul's second letter to the Corinthian church, chapter 12 verses 7–10. Paul had some sort of medical affliction which is not detailed except to say that it was so bad that it tormented him. This obviously was not a common cold or a stomach upset. It was quite probably a long-term illness which never seemed to be alleviated – Paul called it 'a thorn in my flesh'. Paul pleaded with the Lord to take it from him, to heal him, but, from his close relationship with the Lord, Paul felt God's words to him were the real answer to his prayers. The Lord said, 'My grace is sufficient for you, for my power is made perfect in weakness.' Paul goes on to describe the battle he constantly had with life: 'I will boast all the more gladly about my weaknesses, so that Christ's power may rest on me. That is why, for Christ's sake, I delight in weaknesses, in insults, in hardships, in persecutions in difficulties.' He concludes with those defiant yet triumphant words: 'For when I am weak, then I am strong.'

The same Lord Jesus can speak with you like this, lifting you from depression; sadness; an unhappy marriage; difficulties at school, university and work; and all manner of things that make you feel powerless to do anything about them. His grace is sufficient for you. That's the power of powerlessness!

ROBIN OAKE

CHAPTER 1

HOW REAL IS THIS CHRISTIANITY?

As young constables in the Metropolitan Police, my colleagues and I were directed by our sergeant to keep our eyes and ears open for an intruder – not a burglar, but someone who was imitating a police officer. Several local residents had been visited by a polite, middle-aged, well-spoken gentleman making 'house-to-house enquiries about local burglaries'. He had produced a card which he said was his warrant. I smelled a rat, as did the sergeant – a Metropolitan police officer who was smart and well spoken?!

By chance, I was nearby in Marlborough Hill when a gardener told me that he had seen a man of a similar description call at the home of Bob Monkhouse, the comedian. Mr Monkhouse had opened the door and, after a very short conversation, had shouted at the man to 'clear off'. From the gardener I was given the direction in which the man had disappeared, and it wasn't long before I saw him in the distance, in Springfield Road, where I knew other celebrities lived.

I caught up with the man at a front door, which a maid was opening. As I was in uniform, there was no need to introduce myself. The man stammered something about being at the wrong house even before I spoke. Yes, he was the man we were after. Yes, he was respectably dressed and well spoken, pretending to be a police officer, with a forged warrant card in his hand. The weak excuse he gave me was that he was an autograph hunter! In fact, he was a very clever housebreaker.

This was, to all intents and purposes, a police officer to those with whom he conversed. He had that air about him, and many people would have mistaken him for a genuine officer of the law. But, however he acted and whatever the facade, he did not have the power or authority of a properly sworn-in police officer to the point that I did as a qualified officer (albeit in my probationary first two years). I was able to arrest, caution and eventually have him convicted of impersonating a police officer and of the burglaries to which he pleaded guilty.

In the same way, there are those of us who believe we are right with God, that we are Christians and that we are about God's business. But it's a sham. Others may be fooled, but God never is. Galatians 6:7 says, 'Do not be deceived: God cannot be mocked.' The Greek here is 'cannot be sneered at'. So this is a warning. If we recognise our position as a 'pretend Christian' rather than as a 'real Christian', we know that we don't fool God. It is only when we see the sense of being honest with Him that we can sense our place of powerlessness without Him as our Saviour.

Being born again

Jesus is ready always to bring salvation to all who call on Him. To be a follower of Christ means much more than mere attendance at church, either regularly or spasmodically or on special occasions such as Christmas and Easter. No church ritual, no mumbo-jumbo nor any other ceremony has the power or the authority to translate one's ordinary life into that of a Christian. The powerlessness of the 'church' is often down to pew-fillers who regularly attend, in whatever denomination, because it is the thing to do, or because they have been brought up to do it by their parents. Consequently to them it is a ritual that achieves no more than a 'tick in the register' that they were there on Sunday. They engage in no mission to others, have no concern that others might need to be converted and exhibit no real sense of worship or motivation.

We might know that there is something amiss with our lives – that things are not quite as they should be. But we deceive ourselves if we think going to church, turning over a new leaf or making a New Year resolution and so on should make a difference. Through sheer hard work there may be a temporary change, but it doesn't last.

Are you trying to change your own life? Have you asked Jesus to change you?

To become a Christian includes, firstly, a recognition that we fall far short of God's perfect standard. The Bible teaches that God is holy – He is totally pure. But as we read on through the Bible, it shows us that we are not like this. We've all done wrong, and fall short of God's perfect standard. The Bible calls it 'sin'. We don't like to admit it, but if we are honest we know we are unworthy and by our own efforts we cannot be any better.

Yet there is far more to it than that. We must recognise that we need rescuing too. Sin is our essential nature – – it effects every human being, right from the beginning of time (you can read about it in the book of Genesis, chapter 3). There is a famous verse in Isaiah 53, verse 6, which explains: 'We all, like sheep, have gone astray, each of us has turned his own way'. We are nothing except full of sin (Romans 3:10–12) and this has big consequences with God. Ephesians 2:1 tells us that we are 'dead in [our] transgressions and sin'.

We deserve God's punishment – judgment and death. We are living under sin's penalty of eternal damnation (Hebrews 9:27). The New Testament actually calls us 'objects of wrath' (Ephesians 2:3) and 'God's enemies' (Romans 5:10). It's not comfortable reading, but it's vital we do something about it. This is where God provides us with a wonderful answer ... the story does not need to end there.

As John 3:16 tells us, 'For God so loved the world that he gave his one and only Son that whoever believes in him shall not perish but have eternal life.' We deserved God's punishment for our sin but instead God has laid on Jesus, His perfect Son, the 'iniquity of us all' (as prophesied in Isaiah 53:6). When Jesus died, He died for the ungodly – us; 'God demonstrates his own love for us in this: While we were still sinners, Christ died for us' (Romans 5:8).

Provided we turn to Christ in repentance and trust in His finished work for us upon the cross, we are forgiven. We are also 'born again' as God Himself comes to live within us by His Spirit. We can enjoy eternal life with God as part of His family! As the apostle Paul says in 2 Corinthians 5:17: 'if anyone is in Christ, he is a new creation; the old has gone and the new has come!' It is a free gift. Jesus is our righteousness, holiness and salvation (1 Corinthians 1:30). And it is all because of God's love.

In John's Gospel, chapter 3, we read the account of Nicodemus, who was a learned man and a member of the Jewish Council. Keen to know about Jesus, he came to Him under cover of darkness and Jesus was ready to receive him. And what Jesus said to Nicodemus is an unchanged requirement today for all would-be-believers: 'You must be born again' (3:7).

Nicodemus learned that he had to be born again – being religious is nowhere near the mark, because that is just an outward show. Being born again is a new start, having confessed our sin to God, repented of it and then received His forgiveness. The Holy Spirit, who dwells within us, then renews us.

Not by works

When we are born again, we can begin to live to please God in His power. That is, the power of the Holy Spirit. This is a demonstration of the power of powerlessness – we cannot change ourselves; it is the work of God.

Ephesians 2:8–9 tells us, 'For it is by grace [God's free, unmerited, unearned favour] you have been saved, through faith – and this not from yourselves, it is the gift of God – not by works, so that no-one can boast.' We cannot earn salvation by doing good or by doing anything except repenting of our sin – seeking God's forgiveness and asking the Lord Jesus to come into our life. Just as going as a spectator to a soccer match doesn't make us a footballer, so going to church doesn't make us a Christian.

A new life from Jesus is a gift from God. Have you asked Him for that gift?

I had a middle-aged millionaire come to my house asking, 'How do I become a Christian?' However long I spoke, he just didn't get it. One of his problems was that he thought he would have to give up his wealth, donate it to charity and then start from the beginning. No matter what I said about the main priority being to believe in the Lord Jesus, he wanted Christianity to be bolted onto his way of life instead of believing in and then seeking Jesus' way for him and his money. In fact, he did temporarily make some sort of commitment and, with that, attended church for some months before lapsing back into his comfort zone. Jesus will not intrude into our life, be treated as an unwelcome guest or have His Name in our life without our wholehearted commitment to Him.

Not by inheritance

As a young constable in St John's Wood, I once saw an elderly, fur-clad lady on the other side of the road. She was carrying two shopping bags in one hand and an umbrella and handbag in the other. It was an obvious thing for me to cross the road, assist her with the baggage and see her across a busy thoroughfare. She was very grateful, and I walked with her to her home. Somehow in the conversation, we spoke about Christian faith. I mentioned my fairly new faith in Christ and asked her about hers. She stopped in her tracks and said to me, quite sternly but with a faint smile, 'Young man, you don't need to worry about me. My nephew is the Bishop of Norwich.' It seemed quite absurd to me that when time in eternity begins, she hopes that the Lord will recognise her because of her nephew's high position in the church. Faith in Jesus is personal – a personal decision. We cannot inherit Christianity. It is like saying you become a Christian by being born in a Christian country. That is simply not so!

God is nobody's ancestor. What are your own thoughts on 'spiritual heritage'?

Nothing in Scripture states that Christian faith can be inherited. Yes, there may be good examples of that faith modelled by our parents or even by our grandparents or other members of the family. However, faith comes from our personal acceptance of our need and of Christ meeting that need by His forgiveness.

By power

Paul said, 'I am not ashamed of the gospel, because it is the power of God for the salvation of everyone who believes' (Romans 1:16). It is interesting to know that the word 'power' as used by Paul is translated from the Greek word dunamis, from which the modern world gets its word 'dynamite' – explosive power! Whatever is wrong with us if we think that Christianity is something into which we drift, or which only permeates a part of our life?

God's power is for everyone who believes. So what is this power? He is the Holy Spirit in us who believe so that head acknowledgement is enhanced by heart commitment. Without the Holy Spirit, we are powerless, like a vehicle without fuel or an electric appliance which is not plugged in. Salvation is inextricably linked to the power of the Spirit.

The infilling (or baptism) of the Holy Spirit is not something which stopped many years ago. It is the power promised to us in the book of Acts for all who believe in Jesus. Anyone who is born again – born of the Spirit of God, with their sins forgiven and a new life gained – may be filled and empowered by the Holy Spirit now!

People who desperately look for a change of life are crying out for something new. They will try anything from dieting, to drugs, to drink, to 'New Age' ideas about religion; from working harder at their marriages to working harder at business; from pleasure seeking to pleasing everyone. Many of these things are laudable but not life changing – for long.

But it is in that powerlessness, knowing that we can do nothing by ourselves, that we can discover the power of forgiveness, the power of new life and the power of being born again. Our churches should be overflowing as, with all our imperfections, we completely and utterly depend on Jesus Christ, then know His power of forgiveness and renewal.

Reflection

Conversion is not about trying harder to be better. There is a train of thought that alleges that leading a good life, doing no harm to anybody, being kind and being involved in charity work is being a Christian and earns a place in heaven. But that is not so. We need to have something happen within us that is from God Himself. We are powerless to make ourselves 'good enough'. In Isaiah we read 'all our righteous acts are like filthy rags' in God's sight (64:6). We need to be born again by God.

Action

Do you have a relationship with the Lord Jesus Christ? Do you know your sins are forgiven? If you are not sure, why not ask Him to come into your heart today? If you feel you can, pray the prayer below. Or you might like to read the Gospel of John yourself and see the claims Jesus made about Himself, especially in John chapter 3.

Prayer

Lord Jesus, thank you for dying on the cross for me to take away all my sin. I am sorry for all the things I have ever done wrong to hurt you and other people and myself. I believe you died and rose again. Please come into my heart by your Holy Spirit. Thank you, Lord, that you promise never to leave me or forsake me. I am born again. **Amen.**

CHAPTER 2

FORGIVE OTHERS – EVEN GOD?

To become a Christian, or to be restored from a relationship with Christ from which you have drawn away or gone cold, requires us to seek the forgiveness of God. Throughout ages, the evidence of our God's nature is that He hates sin – the act of people turning their back on Him and disobeying His commands – but is always willing to forgive.

A lost son welcomed home

A good picture of forgiveness is found in the story we know as the parable of the Lost (or Prodigal) Son, which is in Luke's Gospel, chapter 15, verses 11–32. The emphasis is nearly always placed on the son returning home, but I believe the parable should be named after the gracious father. It was he who continually looked for his son's return and, despite the son's squandering and selfishness, his father forgave him when he returned – he was filled with compassion for his son, ran to him, threw his arms around him and kissed him. This is a good picture of how our heavenly Father sees us. He loves us.

He wants fellowship with us. When we come to Him for forgiveness, there are no words of recrimination, just joy.

Have you ever loved anyone so much you know that you would die for them? Do you know how it feels to be restored to someone you love very, very much? Imagine that, then multiply it. That is how God feels about us.

However, the result of non-forgiveness is also outlined by Jesus with the brother in the story who saw what was happening in the celebrations. He was bitter and angry, despising his father and newly found brother.

A full sacrifice for us

In Old Testament days, forgiveness was sought by people sacrificing an animal, usually a lamb. This is also a picture of Jesus and what He came to do when He paid the price for our sin. We see in John's Gospel that Jesus was introduced at the beginning of His earthly ministry as 'the Lamb of God, who takes away the sin of the world!' (John 1:29). Isaiah 53:7 states that 'he [the coming Lord Jesus] was led like a lamb to the slaughter'. He took on Himself the infirmities and sorrow of the world, but 'by His wounds we are healed' (Isaiah 53:4–5).

Jesus died as the Lamb of God sacrificed for the world. Even on the cross, while suffering in desperate, unbearable physical pain and unimaginable depths of emotion, Jesus was able to cry out, 'Father, forgive them, for they do not know what they are doing' (Luke 23:34). Forgiveness requires sacrifice. The greatest example of sacrificial forgiveness is that which Jesus cried out on the cross as He died for the sin of the world. His title 'the Lamb of God' reminds the world that this was the ultimate sacrifice – it was a once-for-all sacrifice (1 Peter 3:18), so there would be no need for any more sacrificial lambs as was frequently required in the Old Testament. We surely can only bow our head and in utter deep gratitude say, 'Thank you, Lord. Your body was broken and your blood was shed – for me.'

Spend a moment reflecting on the enormity of what Jesus has done on the cross – for you.

The example of the Lord's prayer

For years, I have tried to listen intently in church services, evangelistic rallies, Christian Unions, small groups and other Christian gatherings to try to work out which is the most read Scripture. I believe it is Matthew 6:9–13. Here we find the Lord's teaching on prayer, which is introduced by Jesus with these words, 'This, then, is how you should pray'. About halfway through the prayer are these familiar words: 'Forgive us our debts, as we also have forgiven our debtors' (v.13). Many of us have been taught this prayer in our childhood – we have said it together in school assemblies – and it is said in many church services as well as in all manner of other gatherings.

Yet do we, in all truth, realise the impact of 'forgive us ... as we ... have forgiven'? The Lord Jesus was actually saying that we can seek God's forgiveness in the same proportion that we are ready to forgive those who wrong us. In fact, Matthew 6:14–15, so very rarely quoted, state facts which are very stark and challenging. If you read them from The Message (one translation of the Bible), it really hits home: 'In prayer there is a connection between what God does and what you do. If you refuse to do your part, you cut yourself off from God's part.'

These words of Jesus are a real challenge because forgiveness is not a natural response for us. Our nature is to seek revenge and retaliation when we are hurt. But the fact is that with God's strength in us to have our attitude changed, it is possible not only to forgive but also to love our enemies (Matthew 5:43–48). With God's love for us and in us, the impossible is possible.

From experience as a police officer, I understand what it is to be slighted, to be insulted, to be falsely accused, to be physically hurt and to be with those who have a son, daughter, mother or father killed, whether accidentally, by dangerous or foolish driving, or by murder or manslaughter. I have empathy when those who are on the receiving end of such pain feel devastated, do not immediately know how to react, yet want to retaliate in some way.

Yet revenge, hitting back and throwing insults is no release. It only bottles up one's emotions, produces no healing effect but adds to the stress. The times I have witnessed fairly minor disputes where an apology or 'I forgive you' would end the argument! Sadly, rarely does that happen, and two parties find themselves in court, facing each other and possibly a fine. Again, outside court after a hearing, there may be shouts of 'Rot in hell,' 'I'll never forgive you,' 'When you come out, I'll kill you.' The anger and temper – the beast in humankind – is there venting its feelings.

While I once was speaking with Nelson Mandela at a particular event, he said, 'We might think that it is weak not to hit back, but to forgive and be forgiven is far more powerful … Forgiveness liberates the soul and removes fear; that is why it is such a powerful weapon.' How do you feel about this statement?

Two angry men

I was once confronted by two very angry men – both of whom were not drunk but were under its influence – arguing over a scratch and dent in a car. One man was alleging that the other had not seen where he was going in the car park, and the other, in loud threatening tones, was saying that the car was badly parked and so he couldn't help touching it. Having been called to the scene by a supermarket supervisor, I walked across to the men, though neither of whom seemed to take any notice of me as I arrived. In an attempt to quell the noise and nuisance, I suggested, in a loud voice, that they step back before any blow was struck. It took a minute or so for both to cease shouting, so I asked what the dispute was about. They both tried to explain at the same time.

'One of you speak, please,' I said.

It was as if a tyre had deflated, and both men stuttered an explanation. Then one simply muttered, 'Look, I was wrong. I wasn't properly looking. I am so sorry. Here's my card; get it repaired and I'll pay.' It was so amusing to see the other driver's amazed face. He was speechless now, and they shook hands.

Sometime later, when walking my beat, I saw these men again. They were not arguing at all. Remembering me, they said, 'Hello' and explained they had become good friends and had a common hobby of model-making. What a transformation!

What about forgiving God?

I doubt that I could count the number of times in a long police career, and also from watching TV news broadcasts, that I have heard people who have witnessed some kind of tragedy shouting at

God, 'Why?' This happens even without any profession of Christian faith. People believe that God, whoever and whatever they perceive Him to be, creates bad situations; that He singles people out to hurt them, or punishes with pain and suffering. This is not the God I know and trust, but I wholly sympathise with those who shout at Him, 'Why me? Why our family?'

In the Isle of Man, as Chief Constable, I was often confronted with people asking 'Why?', as if I knew the answer. But one dreadful evening I was the one asking for a solution along with a grieving husband and family.

My lovely secretary, Diane, at the end of a busy day, had had a little chat with me and said she hoped I wouldn't retire or move from the Island, because she didn't want to work for anyone else. I had laughed and remarked, 'There are many senior officers much better than me.'

And with that, it was with a bright 'Cheerio!' that she left for home.

I had been fast asleep when the telephone rang at 1:30 a.m. It was Diane's husband, sobbing and finding it difficult to talk.

'Diane has died. It was so sudden. I don't know why. What can I do?'

I was completely shaken. 'How? How did she die? Where?'

'She's just died in bed.'

'I'll come immediately.'

In less than half an hour I was with him. An ambulance had been called, but Diane was already dead. She had asked her husband for some water, and before he had returned from their kitchen with a glass, she had simply stopped breathing.

What does one say to comfort those who mourn? I was asked to speak at the packed funeral – Diane was popular as a sportswoman as well as someone who worked hard in the community, in addition to her job at Police HQ. I spent considerable time in prayer to prepare, but was able to pass on to family and friends alike something that my wife, Chris, and I had learned years before.

Never say to God, 'Why?' as if He were to blame. Why not simply say, 'What now?' In other words, the tragedy has happened. What we need to know is how do we pick up the pieces and begin to live again?

Try asking God, 'What now?' rather than 'Why?'

God does not need to be forgiven! He has promised never to leave us, but we cannot always account for the difficult or the inexplicable things that happen to us. Sadly life is rarely, if ever, free from sadness. But we are told that 'in all things God works for the good of those who love him' (Romans 8:28). More than that, and wonderfully, God is able to deal with any situation as we find our solace in His power of love and comfort (as Romans 8:37–39 so beautifully describes). When tragedy strikes, we feel powerless and often in deep shock, but there is hope through Jesus who promised to be with us always (Matthew 28:20). Yes, it is the power of the powerlessness.

The healing power of forgiveness

To be hurt by anyone, perhaps by words and attitude rather than physically, is awful. A natural reaction is to feel some sort of guilt, in case what has been said is actually true; or to shut oneself away and not speak to anyone; or, worse, to try to retaliate in some way. But revenge is never sweet. My experience tells me that to say, 'I forgive you,' not only takes courage but is also the greatest healing medicine.

There is nothing special about our family. We are ordinary people who trust in God; we worship with others in church on Sundays, and witness when and where we can. When our son, Stephen, who was in the Special Branch, was murdered in a terrorist incident in Manchester, it hit us hard. Yet I had to speak to journalists, who had come to our home on the Isle of Man on a chartered plane to question me about Steve and any details of his murder that I knew. I was also extremely tired, having not slept at all.

The press were actually very kind that morning. I am sure there was no malice at all when one reporter called out, 'What do you think of the man who killed your son?' I had not anticipated that question, and I paused before answering. Before speaking I was actually praying for wisdom, knowing that my reply would be broadcast to a wide audience. Eventually I looked at the questioner and said, quite simply, 'I don't know the man or all the circumstances of the operation, but from my heart I forgive him.' Then I heard another journalist call out, 'You what?' So I repeated what I had said, and then wanted everyone in the room to hear it. More boldly I repeated, 'I forgive him.' Then I added, 'I'll be praying that God will forgive him, too.'

The conference took a different turn then – talking about forgiving a terrorist and so on. I was, I remember, in tears and probably near to breaking down. As the main conference concluded, individual reporters wanted to meet me; cameras were clicking; microphones were thrust in my face; and TV cameras were trying to take preference.

When I was alone again, I knew I had been right. Any thoughts of anger and revenge are wrong and, in fact, imprison us – while forgiveness sets us free. That's exactly what I was now feeling. I was realising that I could now face the facts. I could now be stronger. The healing process had begun even though there were more challenges ahead – seeing Steve in the mortuary, then planning the funeral service and attending it in Manchester Cathedral. The long journey to the crematorium after that and the brief service of commitment were especially hard to bear. Even worse was later attending the two-and-a-half-month-long trial and then the ceremony when unveiling the Memorial Stone outside the apartment where Steve was murdered.

All through these different scenarios, and up to the present day, in my quiet times with God (when I read His Bible and speak to Him) at the start of the day, I pray for the man who was convicted of murdering Steve.

Forgiveness is healing – in the domestic scene with family, with neighbours, in the workplace, in sport and in any other situation. Do you feel you need that healing touch?

Healing, peace of mind and positive thinking came to me from forgiving the murderer. But we need to know that by ourselves we cannot forgive. Only with God's help is it possible.

Forgiveness is sacrifice

To say 'I forgive you' is, in a very real sense, a sacrifice. It is not a normal reaction. If it is meant, rather than it being just words, much thought and weighing of consequences have to be brought to bear before forgiving. Jesus, on the cross, in the midst of sacrifice, called out, 'Father, forgive them, for they do not know what they are doing' (Luke 23:34). Stephen, the martyred apostle, similarly cried out as he was being stoned to death: 'Lord, do not hold this sin against them' (Acts 7:60).

The sacrifice our family bore after Steve's death was partly in taking the ridicule from some quarters who believed it was foolish to forgive a terrorist; 'How absurd!' they declared. There were comments from people in our community who felt it quite wrong that a killer could be forgiven, and even a report that I did it for publicity. But these setbacks were soon forgotten and in any case were from a comparatively small number of people, most of whom did not know us as a family.

What does the sacrifice of forgiveness mean to you?

Perhaps another sacrifice of me choosing to forgive this convicted terrorist might be that because I pray for him every morning, it is a daily reminder of Steve and what happened to him; it is a daily reminder that my daughter-in-law, Lesley, became a widow, that their three children lost their father and that my two daughters lost their brother. But I know the biblical truth that what man meant for evil, God has turned to good (Genesis 50:20). Lesley has fallen in love again and married Jon, who, while he will never be 'Dad' as Steve was, is an excellent stepfather, bringing fullness to the family again and especially to Lesley.

It was, to a point, a sacrifice of time when so many letters were sent to us in the light of Steve's death. Chris, my wife, and I agreed that we would answer every letter where there was an address shown and we found ourselves trying to give replies regarding some of the quite horrific incidents in other peoples' lives. I suppose the majority of the letters concerned children, but many were about spouses and other relatives, and some referred to close friends and neighbours. Most were about premature death through disease, or accidents on the road or at work, or incidents at home, and even included injuries in the Armed Forces.

We could have given trite answers to the 'Why?' we were continually asked – it was a serious illness; it was a horrific accident; and so on – but that is no way to console an aching heart. How much better, in our prayer times, to ask what I have mentioned about: 'Lord, what now?' To say that is to articulate two things. Firstly, 'Yes, Lord, this has happened; what can we learn from it?' Secondly, 'Following this event, Lord, what can you give us and help us to do?'

Remember, when you feel powerless to forgive, God will give the power. Again, there is power in powerlessness!

Reflection

Is there a situation in your life where you are finding it difficult to forgive others, or yourself, or God? Forgiveness is not easy. But it is the key to freedom, and we must remember that when we forgive, God forgives us. Someone has described failure to forgive as pouring a cup of poison for our enemy and then drinking it ourselves. Unforgiveness keeps us locked into the past, into that situation – into that person. We need God's help to 'let go'. When we hold on to unforgiveness, it is ourselves we are hurting.

Action

It might be helpful to read a book such as Father, Forgive or Insight into Forgiveness. Do read Psalm 51 in the Bible – a prayer of repentance.

If you find you are not able to forgive someone (or yourself), ask God to give you His forgiveness for them. You might also find talking to a trusted Christian friend or minister useful.

If you feel you are able to forgive, you could write the name of the person and their 'sin' on a piece of paper, then set it alight as a symbol of letting go of the past ... and moving on.

If you feel you are blaming God for something, rather than ask, 'Why?' do you think you can begin to ask, 'What now?'

Prayer

Lord, I am sorry for my sins. But Lord, I know that I must forgive those who sin against me in order to be forgiven. I am asking you for your power to help me to forgive [name person/s] right now.

{If you can, continue with ...} Lord, I forgive [name person/s]. Help me to walk in that forgiveness from this time on. Please bless [name person/s].

Thank you, Lord, for dying on the cross for me and forgiving me for all my sin. Lord, what now? **Amen.**

CHAPTER 3

I CAN'T OVERCOME MY SINS

Why is it that we human beings have a tendency to do things wrong, to break the law, to ignore the rules, to lie, to cheat, to be immoral? It seems to be easier to do wrong than right, even from the youngest age.

I once had my little finger broken on a bowling green, of all places. Bowls is a non-contact game, played gently on sunny days and where cheering is unacceptable though polite clapping is encouraged for a good shot. Having never tried it before, I thought it would be quite easy to reach and lie near the 'jack' with my roll. Oh, was I mistaken that afternoon at Bramshill Police College. After what they call an 'end', I was attempting to pick up my 'wood', when thud! A wood rolled from another rink trapped my little finger and flattened it, breaking the bones in the process and snapping my wedding ring at the same time.

If you have either played or watched a game of bowls, you will recognise what and why it happened. Each wood, though it looks round and symmetrical, is biased on one side so that its weight pulls the wood. By controlling that wood as it is bowled, a player can curve it on its way to the jack.

I believe this illustrates the bias built into humankind. We too have a bias woven into us that needs to be controlled, but our bias is towards wrong. The underlying problem is that we are all prone to rail one way or another. It doesn't seem to matter how much training we have had, how well educated, poor or wealthy we are, the subtlety of temptation is constantly there.

This is why the Bible is so adamant that 'all have sinned and fall short of the glory of God' (Romans 3:23) or, as The Message puts it, 'it's clear enough, isn't it, that we're sinners, every one of us, in the same sinking boat with everybody else?' (Romans 3:20).

Sin and Satan

While we are forgiven by God for our wrong actions and thoughts when we become a Christian, this doesn't make us immune from further sinning. We still live in the same body and retain its weaknesses. The main difference is that the Lord Jesus makes us aware of sin, or sinful intentions. So we have the choice of seeking His strength to resist temptation, or of rejecting or ignoring His power.

There are obvious wrongs. We have laws which tell us what to do and what not to do. But much temptation comes by subtle means. Our thought life is particularly difficult to control. When we see something obscene or impure in a magazine, newspaper or advertisement, we should throw down the paper and turn away from the advert – but even if we do, our thoughts are still prone to wander back.

When you are watching a film or TV programme that shows or promotes something which does not honour God, what do you do?

Our enemy, Satan, is clever and will do anything to undermine the Christian man, woman or young person. We live in a corrupt world and are tainted by what we see and hear. Purity seems to be an anathema to most people and, in their eyes, a weakness. As the Bible depicts him, 'the god of this age' (2 Corinthians 4:4) is 'like a roaring lion looking for someone to devour (1 Peter 5:8) or 'masquerades as an angel of light', deceiving us (2 Corinthians 11:14).

Overcoming the devil is impossible in our own strength. We, by ourselves, are powerless to withstand his attacks, in whatever form they arrive. It is when we admit our position and recognise that the power from our Lord Jesus is at hand, that victory is possible. Even then, because we have resisted temptation, Satan allows pride to permeate our brain – and pride comes before a fall, as well we all know.

Scripture and the devil's lies

Paul, in chapter 7 of his letter to the Romans, outlines for us the situation which we all face:

> *... what I want to do I do not do, but what I hate I do. And if I do what I do not want to do, I agree that the law is good. As it is, it is no longer I myself who do it, but it is sin living in me ... I have the desire to do what is good, but I cannot carry it out. For what I do is not the good I want to do; no, the evil I do not want to do – this I keep on doing ... What a wretched man I am! Who will rescue me from this body of death? (vv. 15–24)*

Paul gives the answer immediately: 'Thanks be to God – [who delivers me] through Jesus Christ our Lord! (v.25). It is to Jesus we look in our powerlessness to resist temptation. He was tempted as we are, yet was without sin (Hebrews 4:15). At the start of His ministry, we see that Jesus resisted temptation by quoting Scripture (Matthew 4:1–11). We must do that, too; God's Word is the sword of the Spirit, effective against the enemy, as Ephesians 6:17 tell us.

How well do you know your Bible? Do you know it well enough to counter the attacks of the enemy?

So, then, the powerlessness of failing under temptation can be translated into a tangible power of resistance by a thorough knowledge of the Bible.

Life is full of temptation. Without the power of God, we are powerless to resist and fight it. Yet the Spirit in us alerts us to the alluring temptation so that we can immediately seek His wisdom, His strength and His way of escape. Paul says in the book of Ephesians that we should 'be strong in the Lord and in his mighty power' (6:10). He goes on to outline the whole armour of God (vv. 13–18) so that we can stand against the devil's schemes – 'For our struggle is not against flesh and blood, but against the rulers, against the authorities, against the powers of this dark world and against the spiritual forces of evil in the heavenly realms' (v.12). We are commanded to 'resist the devil' in James 4:7, for when we submit ourselves to God, the evil one will flee from us.

Of course, one of the devil's lies is that we may not be found out. The Bible refers to 'sin's deceitfulness' (Hebrews 3:13) and obviously if there is hope that our wrongdoing can remain hidden, it becomes more alluring. However, we cannot deceive God. Eventually it is with Him whom we have to deal.

Do you have 'hidden sin' in your life? What do you intend to do about it?

Slavery of addiction

One particular area where we might cry, 'But I can't do it!' is if we are in the grip of an addiction. We will all be conscious of the slavery that addiction brings to one's life. But it is in that powerlessness, knowing that we can do nothing by ourselves, that we can discover the power of Christ.

I know of a Christian family who moved into an inner-city neighbourhood as a deliberate and positive intention to reach people for Christ. Soon after settling into their two-bedroom flat, the father came across two guys snorting cocaine outside his front door. Not wanting his kids to see what they were doing, he challenged them to stop and move on. The next thing he knew, his head was smashing on to the concrete floor and blood was seeping from a deep wound, as well as from his mouth and nose. He had been struck, and struck hard. But he managed to say, 'If Jesus shed His blood for me, I can shed blood for you.' Shocked, the two guys fled.

A few days later, one of them returned and told the father: 'I have not forgotten your words. If your God is that real to you, then I want to know Him.' The assailant was crying out for help. His victim, whose head was still swathed in bandages, gently pointed out that anyone who wanted to believe in Jesus could experience a complete change in their life. The vicious drug abuser sobbed his way into the kingdom of God and was in time delivered from his addiction.

When we think of addictions, we probably think of drugs or alcohol. But there are so many other addictions which grip and deprave lives – such as the abuse of sex and especially the lure of pornography, which destroy happy marriages and lovely relationships. Then there are the workaholics, who are often the cause of ruin in many homes.

There are very commendable counsellors, groups and other secular aids which can offer a way out, and many will follow those paths. But the power of total and lasting deliverance is found in Jesus – who is 'not wanting anyone to perish, but everyone to come to repentance' (2 Peter 3:9). Genuine repentance is the end of play-acting and the beginning of a real-life drama. Picture an addict as someone trapped at the bottom of a chasm, wallowing in deep water and mud. The trapped person has to yell, 'Help me! I'm trapped. I can't get out.' Confession is admission that the addict is in real trouble. If that is not recognised, there will be no rescue. Yet with that admission, Jesus is the divine Rescuer. He has come down into the chasm. He is there alongside the alcoholic, the drug or sex addict and all who are helpless and powerless. The almighty power is in Jesus.

Be honest with yourself. Is there an addiction in your life that you know you are powerless to deal with?

Jamie grew up in a loving family. He was intelligent but a loner. Then he began to fraternise with some low characters whose lives were absorbed in drink and petty theft. Jamie left home, became an alcoholic and then sank into illicit drugs. He was eventually arrested for being an accessory to murder and was imprisoned for six years. When he was released, he slipped back into his old ways. Yet he knew he needed help. He came across a Christian organisation called the Stauros Foundation and in his desperation cried out to God for healing. He heard the gospel message, was willing to confess his sinful life and repent of it, and was born again. He returned home and, although not initially welcomed by his parents, by his persistence and by showing that he really had changed, they came to receive him. Sadly, his mother was diagnosed with cancer soon after, but Jamie spent time with her and was completely restored into the family.

He then applied for and was received as a student for Bible college training. Yes, there really is power in powerlessness.

Life-changing power

We discussed earlier the power of God that is released to us through what is known as baptism or the infilling of the Holy Spirit. This is not an event which occurs when we are 'christened' or baptised as children but when we are saved by making a personal commitment to God. We receive the Spirit of Christ when we are born again 'from above' (see John 3:3–8).

When the first believers were empowered by the Spirit, this encounter was accompanied by the gift of speaking in other tongues (Acts 2:1–13; 10:44–47), as had been prophesied in the Old Testament (Joel 2:28–29). 1 Corinthians 12 tells us that today 'each' believer is given a gift or gifts from the Holy Spirit 'for the common good' (v. 7), that is so that we can act as different parts of the same body – the body of Christ – making a 'team' for Christ. Ephesians 5:18 exhorts us to 'be filled with the Spirit'. Being filled with the Spirit is the power for an effective Christian life – effective in living for Christ and in overcoming all kinds of temptation, as well as in powerfully sharing the good news about Jesus with others. Jesus never gives any of us an impossible task, and it is only by the Spirit's enabling that we are able to fulfil His great commission to preach the gospel to all humankind (Matthew 28:18–20; Acts 1:8).

Examine yourself and see if your Christianity is powerless. Do you desire to meet with God and know the explosive power of His Holy Spirit in your daily living?

I was introduced to a minster in the Church of Wales who had been invited to the annual meetings of the Christian Police Association by a colleague of mine. I liked his company, and he seemed relaxed with us. Then, some weeks later, the minister telephoned me and told me a rather startling story:

> *I had never been converted. I went to theological college and was able to pass through with little problem. I served a number of churches before coming to London and, while I had a good congregation, nothing exciting or out of the ordinary happened. I got my salary, I preached an academic sermon each week and I visited members of the congregation when they were in need. Then as I listened to the men and women at that Christian police meeting, I realised they had something I hadn't got – a real and tangible faith.*

The minister went on to say that he, with others, simply bowed his head at the end of a service and 'did something extraordinary – I prayed that God would touch my life. I confessed my utter need, and my stupidity of being a minister without being a Christian. I know that, for the first time, I really received Christ into my life, and I began at last to realise the power of God in His Holy Spirit.'

It took much courage, he confessed, to stand in the pulpit the next Sunday and tell his congregation what had happened. Some were flabbergasted; a few came and shook his hand and prayed with him. Soon others were being changed, were being converted, and there was a new spirit in worship and then in outreach. Sadly, though, some of the congregation went to worship elsewhere when they began to see the work of the Holy Spirit in this 'new' man.

Extreme weaknesses

God is pure and cannot abide or condone wrongdoing, whether in thought or in action. That is why the Bible concentrates so much on God's purity and His endeavours to show us how wrong sin is. '[God's] eyes are too pure to look on evil; [he] cannot tolerate wrong', Habakkuk 1:13 explains, hence that haunting cry from the cross where Jesus was dying and bearing the intolerable weight of the sin of the world: 'My God, my God, why have you forsaken me?' (Matthew 27:46). Our perfect God had to turn His head away from His Son because He could not look on all our sin that had been placed on Jesus.

It is an awful fact that all humankind is born with sin. It is inherited and cannot be denied. No one has to be taught to do or think wrong things – it is as natural as breathing. So this is our extreme weakness. We are actually born separated from God and without hope, in the sense that we have to find God and trust Him to deal with this inbuilt weakness.

Yet we do have hope because, as John 3:16–21 says:

> *God so loved the world that he gave his one and only Son [Jesus], that whoever believes in him shall not perish [the automatic end for unforgiven sin] but have eternal life. For God did not send his Son into the world to condemn the world, but to save the world through him. Whoever believes in him is not condemned, but whoever does not believe stands condemned already because he has not believed in the name of God's one and only Son.*
>
> *This is the verdict: Light has come into the world, but men loved darkness instead of light because their deeds were evil.*

Everyone who does evil hates the light, and will not come into the light for fear that his deeds will be exposed. But whoever lives by the truth comes into the light, so that it may be seen plainly that what he has done has been done through God.

People often don't recognise their need, or their weakness or their powerlessness, so perhaps they consider themselves to be 'right with God' by relying on the fact that they have not committed any crime, are not adulterers and so on but are going about doing good. But it's not about our own efforts. They won't save us, because they are never good enough for a perfect God. Instead we must realise we are in a muddy, filthy pit and know we need to cry out for help – because we need 'something' that is beyond ourselves as all our best efforts aren't good enough. We must admit we have failed – we can't rescue ourselves and we are too weak to stand against our temptations or addictions. Only then will we cry out to God and find His Son is alive and willing to give us power to live a new life. His power.

Reflection

It is said that an alcoholic, or a drug abuser or a lover of pornography will never actually lose the inner temptation to return to their weakness, rather they turn their life over to Christ, who is able to give power and strength to overcome the strongest of temptations. Spend some time thinking about areas in your own life that might be strongholds of the enemy, where you simply don't have the power yourself to overcome them.

Action

Sit quietly in a place you know you won't be disturbed for a while. Read Psalm 139. You are 'fearfully and wonderfully made' (v. 14); you are unique and special. Read Isaiah 41:10. Imagine Jesus sitting with you. He knows your areas of weakness. Also read Philippians 4:13 and 2 Corinthians 12:9. Though we are weak, we can be empowered by God. Soak in the fact that God loves and does not condemn all who trust in Jesus, and can set them free (Romans 8:1 and John 8:36). Then look at the prayer below and see if you can either pray it on your own or with a trusted Christian friend. (If you are struggling with serious areas of addiction, contact your minister or someone you trust and share your struggles with them. It is important to have ongoing support and accountability to someone who knows the Lord, knows you and understands.)

Prayer

Lord Jesus, your Word says, 'if the Son sets you free, you will be free indeed' (John 8:36). I know I need your freedom in this area [name area] and I confess that I cannot set myself free. I repent of [name any known sin] and thank you for your blood shed on the cross for me. Lord, I am relying on you to give me your power to live to please you. Please baptise me in your Holy Spirit, fill me full to overflowing. Thank you, Jesus. **Amen.**

CHAPTER 4

I FEEL SO STRESSED

Stress is not abnormal; it is a part of life. With regard to structures, stress is basically a tension or a pressure exerted on an object. For instance, a suspension bridge has a tolerable stress on the pillars, the wires and the roadway. Likewise, every building should have been designed to withstand the stress of wind and weather, as well as the weight of people or objects within and on that structure. These two simple examples show that stress can indeed be natural, and problems only occur because of errors by the designer or the builder.

However, we all grow up feeling some kind of stress that makes it harder not easier to deal with our circumstances. Shy and quiet children take time to settle at school, and it can be a while before they come to terms with the anxiety of being away from home, meeting teachers and mixing with others in the class. There are many of us who find it hard to walk into a room, a party or a conference where we don't know anybody. Another common cause of pressure is travelling, whether it's by rail and involves having to change trains;

by air and requires getting to the airport in time; or by car and the fear arises of getting lost or being intimidated by other vehicles on a motorway. Then there is the stress of peer pressure at school, university or in the workplace – the pressure from so-called friends to go binge-drinking; the peer pressure of promiscuity; the pressure of compromise to please the boss ...

Identify an area of stress in your own life. Where are you feeling the most pressured?

The importance of prayer

I mention these examples of stresses and strainings because they are commonplace. They are not trivial to those who suffer, but can be overcome by prayer and by allowing the strength and wisdom of our God to permeate into our life as we spend time with Him.

Many people speak of having a 'quiet time', a time when they look at the Bible and pray. Often they do so as the day starts but some will have such devotions at other times of the day or evening. I prefer to start the day with worship, Bible reading and prayer by getting up early when it is unlikely that there will be any interruptions. I not only enjoy the Bible study and going through my diary of those I would like to pray for, but I also look ahead and anticipate what stresses there will be that day.

That quiet time is not the only time of prayer during a typical day. The Bible urges us to never cease to pray (Ephesians 6:18) and I like to practice that as far as is humanly possible. I speak with God throughout the day. What a difference it makes.

I find public speaking a really large, looming stress. Although I have had Lay Preacher training and a six-month course on public speaking, the nervousness of standing up in front of people has never left me. I was on a preaching circuit with the Christian Police Association even before I joined the Metropolitan Police, and through this I responded to frequent calls to join a witness team to give my testimony or speak at churches. As a police officer, I doubt I could count the number of times I have given evidence in Magistrates' or Crown Courts, even at the Old Bailey. As a senior officer in the Metropolitan Police, in Greater Manchester Police and in the Isle of Man Constabulary, I have had to speak at public meetings and also address politicians and the respective police authorities. I have been behind the table at press conferences and so on ... But the nerves always kick in, a sweat breaks out and quite often I have an upset stomach. Many times when I am waiting to give a speech, I find myself wondering, 'What am I doing here? Why me?'

Some years ago, I and two colleagues, as a Christian Police witness team, went to take the evening service at a small but packed church in New Eltham, south-east London. As we talked in the vestry before the service and I gave a final briefing to my colleagues, I suggested we pray together. One of them prayed, 'Lord, give us nerves so that we rely on you and not on ourselves!' This brought a smile to my face and I said out loud, 'He has answered that prayer long before you asked!'

While there are many situations in which we experience a 'natural' fear, our need for peace in them is always met by prayer. Jesus promised us His own peace (John 14:27). Sometimes, I may experience a fragile peace which, if I take my mind off the Lord, will be broken, but He is there, He is upholding me and He is giving me strength. Indeed Jesus invites us to give Him all our anxieties: 'Do not be anxious about anything, but in everything, by prayer and petition, with thanksgiving, present your requests to God. And the peace of God, which transcends all understanding, will guard your hearts and your minds in Christ Jesus' (Philippians 4:6–7).

God is the power-answering God who knows our inner fears and weaknesses. It is in powerless situations that the power of our God can be manifested.

Are you anxious today? Can you bring that anxiety to the Lord now?

Jesus told us not to worry but to trust that God knows all our needs (Matthew 6:25–34). We should always cast our cares on Him (1 Peter 5:7). That is the way of peace in our day-to-day lives. But sometimes we find ourselves in the crisis of overwhelming stress.

Times of overwhelming stress

In the Bible, we read of King David, who spent much of his life dealing with one very real crisis after another. In Psalm 31, verses 1 and 3, he says, 'In you, O LORD, I have taken refuge; let me never be put to shame ... you are my rock and my fortress, for the sake of your name lead and guide me.' Here is a man wholly committed to God, trusting Him and walking with Him, and recognising how good God is to him and how He is the solid foundation of his faith. David knew that as he faced each day, his strength was in God. He was confident in stating that his refuge was in God. God was his rock and fortress, and that would guide and lead him through the perils of life – even though David knew more than most about overwhelming stress.

Stress is nothing of which to be ashamed. Each of us has pressure to face every day, but in Psalm 31 we see a strong believer under immense stress. Verse 9 says, 'Be merciful to me, O LORD, for I am in distress; my eyes grow weak with sorrow, my soul and my body with grief.' David is utterly drained, physically and emotionally (v. 10) and all his friends appear to have abandoned him (vv. 11–12). He feels slandered and knows that there is a conspiracy against him (v.13).

Those who do not have faith in God may share their problem with a reliable friend; they may relax with some alcohol; they might take their stress out in the gym or in their sport; some have sessions with a stress counsellor. None of these are wrong or harmful, but they are not the ultimate answer. Friends are not always as reliable as we may think and their advice may not always be wise or viable. Alcohol can lead to dependence. Overindulgence in the gym or sport can have harmful effects on the body if it is not done under supervision. Sessions with a counsellor certainly can be beneficial but also may cause dependency. And because none of these is the best answer, and our stress plays more and more on the mind, tragedy and disaster may follow.

How did David, a man of God under severe pressure, cope? Psalm 31:14 tell us: 'But I trust in you, O LORD; I say, "You are my God". My times are in your hands ...' The rest of the psalm is a triumph of confidence in God and in His wonderful love.

Sometimes, whatever it is we are called to handle seems impossible. It is then that we find the God of the impossible waiting to take care of us.

Jesus is the best answer to all our worries. Do you believe that?

The power of powerlessness is so clear in the Lord Jesus. Yes, He is God in the flesh (Colossians 2:9) but Philippians 2 tells us that He humbled Himself, He made Himself nothing, taking the nature of a servant (vv. 6–8). He was obedient to His Father's call to die in our place, even though He cried out for 'this cup' to be taken from Him (Luke 22:42). At this point, Luke's Gospel tells us that 'his sweat was like drops of blood falling to the ground' (Luke 22:44). That surely is the extremity of stress.

Jesus seemed powerless before Pilate and Herod, then before the Roman guards as they nailed Him to the cross. Yet Jesus became powerless deliberately so that you and I might live; He died for the world. Moreover, his supreme example of power coming from powerlessness is in fact transferred to us – if only we would receive it.

Stress and money

There are many areas we might examine for particular signs of stress in our lives, such as sickness and loss (see chapters 9 and 10), and the brittle nature of relationships in this promiscuous age, with adultery, divorce and their accompanying guilt and ongoing family issues. Another place where we may find ourselves in extremities of stress is in the area of finance. With our current economic problems, unemployment, redundancy and escalating debt, surely none of us remain completely untouched by this, so it's a subject that is worth exploring here.

Aren't churches after your money?

You may have heard the comment, 'I won't come to church because they're always asking for money!' There is some truth in this, especially where the building is an ancient edifice which needs constant care and attention merely to keep it standing.

I was playing golf with three good friends at Port St Mary in the Isle of Man when one of them asked me about the cost of our church's new building: 'How much was the budget?' I quickly answered that, simply because I knew as the chair of the Trustees. But the next question puzzled me for a moment: 'How are you raising that sort of cash? Churches usually have a "temperature gauge" outside showing what has been raised and how much further the giving has to go.'

My answer rather surprised my friend: 'We pray for it.'

'You what?' said one of the others.

'We pray for it,' I repeated.

My friends obviously stewed on this for the rest of the round, for when we arrived at the prize-giving, one of them stood up and announced, 'Robin said something amazing about his church this morning – about raising money. Why don't you tell us all about it?'

So I stood in the midst of my golfing friends and spoke about the prayer life of the church, trying not to major just on the raising of money but testifying about the bounteousness of our God. However, I must add that sadly within our church family there is a problem with some people's attitude to finances. Our church secretary once announced to the congregation: 'I have good news for you today. We have sufficient money to pay for the new building. The sad news is that it is still in your wallets and pockets!'

Yet in 2 Corinthians 9:7 we read 'Each man should give what he has decided in his heart to give, not reluctantly or under compulsion, for God loves a cheerful giver.' This is a good reason not to be miserly.

We also learn much from Jesus' commendation of the widow in Luke 21:

> *As he looked up, Jesus saw the rich putting their gifts into the temple treasury. He also saw a poor widow put in two very small copper coins. 'I tell you the truth,' he said, 'this poor widow has put in more than all the others. All these people gave their gifts out of their wealth; but she out of her poverty put in all she had to live on' (vv. 1–4).*

But what else does the Bible say about our finances – apart from not trusting in them (Luke 12:13–21) or loving them (1 Timothy 6:10)? And how can giving regularly alleviate stress?

The blessing of tithing

The biblical blueprint for giving is quite simple – you should tithe or, in plain English, put aside a minimum of a tenth of one's income and give it to God (see Leviticus 27:30–33). The promise of God is that what is given to God in this way is repaid by Him with such blessing that it cannot be contained (Malachi 3:10).

Our pastor once spoke about finances and expounded the biblical truths on it, starting with the tithe. It was most helpful but very challenging to my wife and me, as on a constable's salary and that of a nurse, we only just had enough to manage on ten-tenths, let alone reducing that to nine-tenths. We prayed about this and mentioned it to our pastor, who understood where we were coming from, but then quoted from Malachi 3: '"Test me in this," says the LORD Almighty' (v. 10). 'He won't let you down,' the pastor told us, confidently. 'You'll be amazed.' So we began to put aside one-tenth of our joint incomes by opening another account which would only be spent on Christian work – we name it 'The Lord's Account' – and we have never looked back. The tenth was the starting point and the absolute minimum, but as you would expect God has kept his promise of blessing.

We know of widows on small pensions, couples who have few pennies to rub together, school children who receive little pocket money and others who have learned to give one-tenth to the Lord's work. Who are we to withhold all that we earn or receive? Our God, the creator of the universe, has given us everything by sacrificing His beloved Son's life. And He is Jehovah-Jireh (Genesis 22:14) which means, 'the LORD will provide'. No matter how much we give, we cannot out-give God. If you have stress-related issues regarding money, simply try tithing.

How strong is your faith in the promise of God to 'meet all your needs according to his glorious riches in Christ Jesus' (Philippians 4:19)?

Let go!

When a non-swimmer goes down into the water, he doesn't have time for play-acting. He can only shout, 'Help – save me!' because he has no other means of saving himself. He is at his weakest. And then, by stopping his struggling and clinging to his rescuer, he is saved. Likewise, in the depths of our despair, God can give us power. Indeed, the trick is to really let go and let God when life threatens to overwhelm us.

To trust someone, you have to know them. When you know Jesus, and realise He can be trusted, then it becomes easier to let go of stressful issues and trust Him with them. Often we try hard to 'make things work' to the point of exhaustion before surrendering to Him. Remember, although some kind of stress is normal, at extremes it can overpower us unless we recognise the symptoms and yield it all to our God. Stress can ruin a life; it can cause mental illness, break families and make us do irrational things such as attempting suicide. Specialists, counsellors and psychologists can be of enormous help, but the ultimate healing is found in Christ alone. Jesus said: 'Come to me, all you who are weary and burdened, and I will give you rest. Take my yoke upon you and learn from me, for I am gentle and humble in heart, and you will find rest for your souls. For my yoke is easy and my burden is light.' (Matthew 11:28–29).

So give up, give in, recognise your weakness and yield it to the Saviour. At our weakest, in the depths of despair, God gives power. As 2 Corinthians 12:9 says, 'My grace is sufficient for you, for my power is made perfect in weakness. Therefore I will boast all the more gladly about my weaknesses, so that Christ's power may rest on me.'

Reflection

'Look at the birds of the air; they do not sow or reap or store away in barns, and yet your heavenly Father feeds them. Are you not much more valuable than they?' (Matthew 6:26). As you reflect on this verse, think of how precious you are to God, and how much He cares for you.

Action

Try to make space for a daily 'quiet time', if you don't already have one. This can be a great way to combat stress. Again I say that first thing in the morning is preferable, when we can bring all our concerns for the day to the Lord in prayer. You might like to find a regular spot where you can read the Bible and bring your worship, thanks and requests to God. Perhaps use daily Bible study notes, or light a candle if you like. If you can, imagine putting particular worries

in a box and handing them to Jesus. Trust God to provide for, guide and lead you.

Prayer

Gracious Father God, I thank and praise you that you love me and you care about everything that happens to me. You know all my anxieties and worries and you ask me not to bear them alone, but to give them to you, the One who can work it all out. Thank you for your love, your patience, your perfect timing and your guidance, Lord. **Amen.**

CHAPTER 5

BULLYING, OSTRACISM AND NOT BEING PART OF THE CROWD

School was never a drudge to me; even primary school was fun. The masters and mistresses at the latter were excellent teachers and with patience and good humour gave me an excellent foundation for secondary education.

One of my lasting impressions from my secondary school was the care and specific attention given to some of my fellow school chums who came from very poor homes and thus wore the distinctive clothes of poverty, suffered from malnutrition and had unwashed, matted hair. The staff were careful to spend time with them and give them special consideration, without making them feel awkward or ashamed. Nevertheless, those from badly off homes were embarrassed to change in the same cloakroom for games and sport because their underwear was ragged and worn with holes. I suppose those of us children who came from homes where the dad was working and poverty wasn't an issue used to feel pity for them, but I hope not derision ... even in our tender years. I had two friends who were in this awful position, which meant that I was never invited to their homes – though my parents made a point of inviting them to our home in Hooley. I am sure it didn't cross my mind that such friends were different.

But then I passed the eleven-plus exam and went on to the local grammar school where, in this respect, things were quite different. One lad in the first form was sent home for having dirty clothes; another was given detention because his shoes were not clean! They were from poor homes and, while I knew that their respective fathers were out of work, as some had been since returning home from the war, I felt shame for those lads though I didn't at first know what to do about it. But that wasn't all.

School uniform was a blazer, grey trousers, a white shirt and the school striped tie ... for the majority of us. So what about the others? I suppose about thirty boys were in grey suits, with the school badge sewn on to the front pocket of their jackets, and grey shirts, some of whom had school ties but not all. Also their sports clothes were dull grey vests and shorts. I discovered that they were from a local children's home and this was their uniform. Sadly, it distinguished them from fellow students, whose clothes were bought from the outfitters in the town.

You may wonder why I take time to mention this. I do so because inscribed on my memory is the attitude of some masters at the school towards many of the lads from the children's home and, I am very sad to say, the bullying which occurred from time to time that was vented by those from 'normal' homes. For example, I remember the snide remarks from one master about the poorly prepared homework by boys from the children's home. When they tried to explain how difficult it was to find a quiet and undisturbed place to read or write, they were given detention for answering back! I also feel a sense of guilt about those times when fellow students would strip a 'home' boy naked; of home boys not being selected for sports teams because they couldn't obtain the proper team colours, and were thereby ridiculed; and of home boys who had no particular friends or were forbidden to attend a birthday party in the evening as it would be 'out of hours'.

In a sense, I am only skirting round the underlying and dreadful things that these home boys had to endure. I have stopped short of describing the many instances of cruelty which they suffered. I might add that when one or two of us drew all this to the attention of Form or House Masters, very little or nothing was done to prevent such attitudes. So it would seem to be yet another of those powerless situations. But was there any way out of it? Could there be any power?

Perhaps I was slow to recognise what was going on, but in my teens I became a Christian and it soon touched my conscience that the home boys were so disadvantaged. When the lads at school realised that I was changing, that I now had a faith, one of the more senior home boys, David Kingdon, began to take an interest in my welfare. Previously I'd known David only at a distance since he was at the time, I guess, in the sixth form, well ahead of me. Yet he told me one day that he was a Christian, and when he knew that I had been converted, he and other Christians in the school began to encourage me. It was during one of those Christian Union informal meetings that David opened up about the attitude that he and others from the home daily experienced.

David's calm and assured comment was so simple: 'I pray for them!' Up till a few months previously, prayer to me had been what was read from a book in church. I had no conception about daily prayer times and being able to pray for others in any situation outside of church. Therefore David's positive attitude firstly baffled me. Then, because I could see in him a cheerful, head held high, which was not in any way an artificial poise, I recognised that this was the Christian's response to anyone who made life so difficult for those who, for no fault of their own, were living in a children's home. I believe it gave me the courage to try and follow his attitude and even defend my friends from the home. Yes, their grey-suited uniform always made them identifiably different, but beneath the exterior they were flesh and bone like me. Unlike many of them who were from broken homes or fatherless families or for many other reasons were living in the home, I had a stable upbringing, but I needed to change my attitude.

David eventually became Deputy Head Boy; I wonder if he would have been Head Boy if he were given a school uniform? His Christian life was well known throughout the school. Though he bore the brunt of undeserved stigma on behalf of those who lived alongside him, he actually was closely following the life of the Lord Jesus who Himself was despised and rejected and familiar with suffering (Isaiah 53:3).

When I met David some time later, he had become a Baptist minister, obtained a Master of Arts and then, ultimately, been appointed Principal of the Irish Baptist College in Belfast. This was the life of a boy once vilified in his grey suit and shirt and powerless to do anything about it except in the power of the Lord Jesus.

I have only mentioned one form of mental torment here but I have to ask you whether you know of such behaviour and what your attitude is towards it? Ostracism is an evil form of bullying. Prejudice is another that is still prevalent in many areas of life.

You see, on a completely different plain, many people within our communities are similarly suffering. It may be because of their colour and race, their different religion, their dress or their problems with the English language. Others, even though they may have played a part in their plight, suffer because of their drug addiction, their alcoholism or their homelessness. Who are we to judge because they are so different from us?

Such folk may be finding it very difficult to make ends meet; they may find it impossible to get or hold down a job. Perhaps they tolerate the way their life has become without reasoning about it or hearing that there is a way out. Yet it has been truly said that when one is at the bottom, there's always a way up. Jesus Himself said:

> *Are you tired? Worn out? Burned out on religion? Come to me. Get away with me and you'll recover your life. I'll show you how to take a real rest. Walk with me and work with me – watch how I do it. Learn the unforced rhythms of grace. I won't lay anything heavy or ill-fitting on you. Keep company with me and you'll learn to live freely and lightly (Matthew 11:28–30, The Message).*

Reflection

Prejudice of any kind is forbidden in Scripture. Carefully read James 2:1–13 to see how favouritism had begun to erode the early church.

Action

What are the ways in which you need to change your attitude towards people? Resolve not to judge people by their appearance, circumstances or other factors. Remember instead that all people are precious in God's eyes.

Prayer

Heavenly Father, you must be sad to see a world full of strife, bitterness, argument and ill-treatment. You loved this world so much that you sent your only Son, Jesus, whose life portrayed love, forgiveness and grace. He condemned bad attitudes and ridicule. Lord, please help me to follow Jesus more closely and to be prepared to see through the external differences to hearts that need you – so that they too, through my attitude, may turn to you in faith and receive that new life you promised to all who believe in you. In Jesus' name, **Amen.**

CHAPTER 6

SURELY THERE'S NO HOPE FOR THE CRIMINAL?

In my day promotion to the highest ranks in the police service involved a three-day stay in Eastbourne with a three-hour written examination, three intelligence tests, time chairing discussions plus interviews with Ministry of Defence officers, senior civil servants and also the top ranks in the police. One of the interviews was an hour with a psychologist. As I walked into a hotel for this interview, the psychologist met me in the foyer and, I suppose as a way of introducing himself and putting me at ease, asked me what seemed a strange question as we walked to the interview room. 'Do you believe, Mr Oake, that a murderer could ever be a priest?'

We sat down and I began to answer that question. As I said, 'Yes, it could be possible,' the discussion got much deeper. We debated many questions. Would he ever be trusted? Would his congregation accept him? Would he have to continually apologise? Would the police have to be involved and provide a reference? In fact, this topic – a murderer and my Christian faith – was my complete hour-long interview ... and my interviewer was apparently unconvinced! My reply, of course, might have seemed a bit naive, but I firmly believe, on scriptural grounds, that no one is beyond redemption and therefore, if redeemed, can be fully used in the Lord's service.

There was a time when anyone who stole a loaf of bread would be imprisoned and even deported to a far-off country, never to be seen again in the United Kingdom. Things have changed of course over the years and punishments for those found guilty of any crime, minor or serious, have appropriate penalties. The legal system always provides for a defence lawyer in court and carefully prepared reports by, say, the Probation Service are produced if a defendant is found guilty. In theory there are enough safeguards to prevent a miscarriage of justice, although it has to be conceded that the system is not entirely foolproof. Nevertheless, prisons and other such institutions are crowded with men and women who have committed crimes and are serving their punishments. Others have been found guilty but not imprisoned, instead having to pay a fine or serve a period of community service, or else are given an absolute discharge, but still they have the stigma of guilt.

As I said before, no one is beyond redemption and there are a number of agencies which provide help and advice to recalcitrants. Every prison should have its own ministers of whatever religion is represented in that jail. I have known of, and even worked with, Christian ministers in prisons such as Strangeways and Styal.

What no other faith but Christianity can offer is complete healing from whatever crime has been committed with forgiveness in Christ, as well as a new life ahead with the strength of the indwelling Spirit of God. It all starts, of course, at the cross, where

Jesus Himself forgave a repentant thief (Luke 23:32, 39–43). One could recount a huge number of examples since then of convicted men and women who have sought solace from God and found new life in Him, thus experiencing a complete change in their lives, which the Bible calls being 'born again'. I myself have a host of stories of men and women who have been powerless to do anything about their conviction but have found the power of the Holy Spirit in their lives as they yielded to Christ.

For example, I have in mind two men convicted of terrorist offences who were both converted in prison and now have teamed up to preach the gospel together. Another, an armed robber, met with Jesus in his Dartmoor prison cell and, after finishing his sentence, began a life-long dedication to the Lord Jesus in speaking for Him. Two men on opposite sides in World War Two, who were dragooned into army service to kill, discovered years later – after peace was declared – that each had become Christians and now are teamed up together in God's service.

During my first days in the police I often walked the beat down the street where a man lived who was later convicted of child murder and sentenced to life imprisonment. While he was in prison, the chaplain introduced him to a living faith in Jesus. Now a new man, he began to learn with others about the Bible and later started his own Bible study group in the prison. Prison officers could hardly believe their eyes when this man changed so completely.

I think also of a nurse who was convicted abroad of carrying drugs in her luggage and, after a long remand in custody, was sentenced to an inordinately long term of imprisonment. She was so depressed that one day – determined to die – she lay under the kitchen (built on stilts) where the poisonous snakes sought morsels to gore. Incredibly, she was not bitten, and then heard about two elderly ladies who visited a prisoner and talked about Jesus. She met the ladies herself and, after the friendship grew, they introduced her to the Lord Jesus, who came into her life. Some time later she was released during an amnesty and, returning to England, devoted herself to Christian service and helping prisoners to find faith in Christ.

Another example relates to Corrie Ten Boom, a lovely Dutch Christian who, with her sister and parents, was incarcerated by the Gestapo in a concentration camp for helping many Jews to escape the Nazi Holocaust. First her parents and then her sister died in the camp, but some time later Corrie was released – actually through a clerical error by the prison staff! She then devoted herself to continue her Christian witness by speaking of her faith. One day she was confronted by a man whom she didn't recognise but who said he was one of her guards in the concentration camp. He knew of her faith and, cruel though he had been in the extreme at the camp, he had since been converted and wanted to seek her forgiveness. She hesitated but knew that as Christ had forgiven her, so she must forgive this repentant man. As she did, she knew here was a man who unmercifully had ill-treated civilian men and women – and a man who, whatever he felt about the gas chambers, was powerless to do anything about it – but who now had a new power in his life as he repented, sorrowing for his dreadful sins.

So, to return to my interviewer's question, can a murderer become a priest? The answer must be yes, although there needs to be irrefutable evidence of his conversion, much discipling and teaching, and another conviction(!) – a conviction that he has been 'called' to the ministry.

The very sad conclusion to this is that many, many people who are upright, have never been in trouble, have good families, have been employed with an excellent record but have rejected or ignored the offer of salvation from Jesus therefore are actually without hope of new life here on earth or eternal life in heaven. Without turning to Christ, they are powerless.

If we are Christians, how true of many is it that – as if we ourselves are guiltless – we do not pray for those who have committed crimes, have little compassion for them and condemn them in our minds as beyond redemption. Yet in God's view we are just as much sinners and in need of salvation as them – so who are we to point a finger?

Reflection

In prisons, remand centres or mental hospitals many feel that they have hit rock bottom and are powerless to do anything about it. Those that do try to reform find it so difficult with a past that is condemned by so many in society. So we must ask ourselves how much concern we have for such people. Surely none of us like the crimes, whether it be murder, serious assault, theft, rape, child abuse or whatever. Yet like Christ we have an obligation to hate their sin but love the sinner.

Action

How much time, then, do we spend in praying for those in prison, for instance? Consider whether this would be an opportunity to recognise that there is the power of prayer for the powerless and condemned.

Prayer

Lord, I am so fortunate to have been delivered from my past life and had my sin forgiven. Thank you, Jesus, for dying for me and bringing me to seek your love and forgiveness. Help me therefore to see others in a new light and to pray for them that they too might know your forgiveness and receive the new life you offer. **Amen.**

CHAPTER 7

IMPRISONED AND PERSECUTED FOR FAITH

To those of us in the western world, it does seem hard to believe that men and women, children too, who believe in and trust the Lord Jesus have such hard lives that they constantly are under the threat of imprisonment and persecution. But it happens in more places and countries than perhaps we imagine.

The life lived with Jesus is a peaceable one. We are encouraged to love our enemies; pray for those who ill-treat us; be ready to give hospitality; visit the sick and those in prison; be kind to one another; and live a life which serves others. Yet in some countries, pastors of churches, members of their families and those who meet for fellowship are hounded, hated and horribly ill-treated. It does seem to be an anathema. But are those who are so ill-treated powerless to do anything about it?

Wonderfully, in the greatest sense, such persecuted Christians have the power of prayer. Nothing and no one can stop a Christian praying wherever they are incarcerated. No doubt they will pray for one another but they will be praying, too, for their captors and tormentors. The power of prayer is unlimited!

Jesus warned of persecution. He Himself suffered it at the hands of 'religious' leaders and from many others who mocked Him. In His Sermon on the Mount, in Matthew 5, the eighth Beatitude he lists is: 'Blessed are those who are persecuted because of righteousness, for theirs is the kingdom of heaven' (v. 10). As the notes say in the NIV Study Bible, 'The word "blessed" means more than "happy", because happiness is an emotion dependent on outward circumstances. "Blessed" here refers to the ultimate well-being and distinctive spiritual joy of those who share in the salvation of the kingdom of God.'

Jesus also said in John 15:18, 'If the world hates you, keep in mind that it hated me first.' Jesus was able to deal with persecution. So to us He says, 'Love your enemies, do good to those who hate you, bless those who curse you, pray for those who ill-treat you' (Luke 6:27). No power on earth can stop us doing that.

The apostle Paul was previously a well-known and revered (by some) persecutor of Christians, even to the point of condoning murder (see, for example, the stoning of Stephen in Acts 7:54 – 8:1). I wonder how many Christians of that day, perhaps fearing that Paul and his cohorts would discover them, actually prayed for him, and if so what rejoicing there would have been when the news came that he had been converted! That is the power of powerlessness.

This takes us back to the point of this book. I have already quoted from Paul's second letter to the Corinthian church, 12:9–10, where he writes of how God said to him, 'My grace is sufficient for you, for my power is made perfect in weakness ...

That is why, for Christ's sake, I delight in weaknesses, in insults, in hardships, in persecutions, in difficulties. For when I am weak, then I am strong.'

Take the example too of Pastor Richard Wurmbrand, who was imprisoned, beaten, ill-treated, starved and separated from his wife and family for years under the communist regime of Ceausescu in Romania. The deprivations which he suffered were such that it is hard to believe that any human could treat another so cruelly. But Pastor Wurmbrand prayed for his captors in his cold, damp and filthy cell – no one could stop him doing that. Then one day another prisoner was flung in the cell next to his, and Wurmbrand quickly realised that it was one of his former guards who, impressed by Richard's faith, had been converted! Now he too would suffer like the man he had guarded.

Books have been written about similar imprisonments and torture, done by godless, inhumane people. But we serve a wonderful God who states, and it is so true, that He will never leave us or forsake us (Hebrews 13:5). God is sovereign and nothing or no one can thwart Him. The paradox is that the more such individuals persecute Christians, the more and more others follow the Christians' faith so that the church of Christ is growing faster in such countries than anywhere in the world. This has certainly been the case in China, where the number of Christians has skyrocketed despite intense persecution, particularly under Chairman Mao's Cultural Revolution. Yet the persecutors do not see sense or recognise what is going on under their noses …

Christians are never powerless in these situations. However dark it seems, however painful the torture, however heart-rending it is when a husband, mother, or pastor is arrested and imprisoned, however sad for families when a Christian is executed, while it may all seem beyond us, throughout it God is working His purposes out as one year succeeds another. The unseen power of Christ is unstoppable by man whatever the circumstances.

Reflection

I doubt we will have to face such cruelties but we do live in a world, cities, towns and villages where the majority of people do not have faith in Jesus or recognise His love for them. Some have deliberately turned away from Christianity but most – through no fault of their own – have no idea about why Jesus came into the world, that He died for them and that He can give new and eternal life.

Action

How often do we concern ourselves with fellow Christians in other countries who are under threat? Now is the time to rally together in worldwide prayer for the persecuted church. Also pray for all Christians in the United Kingdom, that we would have a strong faith to withstand the works of Satan if we are misunderstood, ostracised or even taken to court because of what we believe and know to be true.

Prayer

Thank you, Father, for loving this world and everyone in it so much that you sent your only Son, Jesus, to live here before dying on the cross. We pray that in knowing our sin is forgiven and we have the certainty of eternal life, we may always be ready to give a reason for the hope we have – even though we may feel a little shy about it. Lord, you faced rejection and we might be laughed at when we speak about you, but we do ask for strength to be different so that at least some may see the difference you make to our life. Help us and remind us to pray for our family, our friends, our neighbours and our colleagues and then not to be tongue-tied when they ask us about our faith. **Amen.**

CHAPTER 8

FAMILIES, FRIENDS AND NEIGHBOURS

Happy families are the greatest source of strength and encouragement. By loving each other, parents love their offspring. When children see their parents loving each other, it brings security to them. Such family commitment to one another is the cement of good relationships, the place to learn good manners, the comforting home where others are welcome and the place where support is found when difficulties arise.

Sadly, I could outline a huge number of families in my experience as a police officer who don't live like that – where husband and wife bicker and have periods of not speaking to each other, or where the husband spends too much time at the pub, club or even continually stays late at work and so on. Even when parents are happy together and try their hardest to teach their children how to live right, problems arise, especially with teenagers. Parents should encourage their children to meet and spend time with appropriate friends because young people tend to pick up the bad habits of their peers.

Hanging out with the gang can mean drinking alcohol to excess, or experimenting with drugs.

Is your family situation a happy one? If it is, thank God. If not, talk to God about this now and ask Him for His peace. Is there a trusted Christian friend you can share this with?

Family problems

Sometimes parents seem powerless to stop children going off the rails. Which parent hasn't experienced a teenager shouting, 'Don't worry! I know what I'm doing. Will you just stop nagging me?' – accompanied by the slam of the front door. Even 'good' church-going families have their problems.

One such instance was with Jamie, whose dad called me in a panic saying, 'Officer, my son is missing. He left home at half past four in a real mood. I've no idea where he's gone. I've tried his mobile but he's not answering; I just don't know what to do.' It was nearly 2 a.m. and fifteen-year-old Jamie had disappeared. Up to a year before this, he was doing well at school, both with his work and in sport. He did his homework religiously and his parents were proud of him. But gradually, over a period of time, he began to change. He spent much more time in his bedroom, not doing homework but on his laptop. His mobile was constantly ringing. He often went out, giving no clue as to where he was going. At a parents' evening, teacher after teacher asked his mum and dad what had come over Jamie. His school work was suffering; he seemed to be in with the wrong crowd; he came to school tired and irritable and was showing signs of aggression.

Because I knew the family, I had spoken with Jamie once or twice in a casual sort of way. As far as I knew, he was not in trouble with the law, but what was he doing in his long hours out of home? He would often come home by about ten at night and avoid his parents by rushing upstairs to his bedroom. But this time it was different.

To cut a long story short, Jamie was eventually found by one of London's tramps, who told a passer-by about a young lad unconscious behind the toilets in Kilburn High Road, lying in vomit and blood. The boy was badly injured about the head and abdomen and was in fact seriously ill, not only from the injuries but also from a drug overdose. Jamie did recover, but he was scarred by all that happened and became a miserable, moody young man who left school prematurely with no good exam results.

The underlying sadness here was that his churchgoing parents were blamed by some neighbours and by most of their respective families for giving Jamie a bad upbringing, overindulging their son and not disciplining him in his early years. Relatives were especially critical, while also doing nothing to help the situation.

At church, however, through all the trauma, the minister and his deacons were wholly supportive, visiting the parents, spending time with them in prayer and so on. The parents were at their wits' end, of course, but they found immense strength from Christian fellowship, in their times at church and in Bible reading and prayer at home. They seemed powerless to do anything but recognised that their boy was not beyond the reach of the Lord Jesus.

That is a sad story but let's not fail to see that, as in the Book of Job, the 'Job's comforters' of close family and friends did nothing to help. Pointing the finger is a dreadful discouragement and their comments just drove the parents into deeper despair. How much better it would have been if instead they had come alongside and consoled Jamie's parents.

Do you ever 'point the finger'? Can you see how harmful it can be?

Through my policing experience in all ranks, I have seen broken families causing dreadful unhappiness, with people driven to attempt suicide and having nervous breakdowns. Most of these situations have arisen because of a bad example being set, family members not listening to, accusing and/or abusing one another, and there being little or no support from family or friends. However, it is not all doom and gloom.

What makes a family?

Primarily, a real family is a set of married parents and their children living together, teaching and learning together, and supporting each other in sickness and in health. These are the bricks which construct and keep a family. But it doesn't always happen. Although some of us have been blessed with strong family ties, not all have. Broken homes and 'blended families' are sadly the norm these days, with all their attendant insecurity. For the children, this may result in a sense of not knowing your place and of transience, which can have a knock-on effect into adulthood. Many people do not bother with marriage at all, and live lives of 'serial monogamy', with children from different partners. Surely this is an unstable way of living and cannot breed security in our offspring.

The real strength of the family is the cement of a personal faith in Jesus Christ, partly because that faith combines all that is good in life, and mostly because it continues through death into eternity. The wider family of relatives, good neighbours and Christian friends are all added stays to the strength of the family. But when you don't have a family unit as such, these people can become the family you are missing. After all, doesn't the Lord promise to put the lonely into families (Psalm 68: 6)? Blood ties make a family. But when we belong to Christ, we become part of His family, because of His shed blood for us. Our identity is found in Him as a son or daughter of the living God (Romans 8:16–17). So fellow Christians become our brothers and sisters; we are one in Jesus (John 17:11).

If you are a Christian, whatever your personal circumstances, you are not an outcast or alone. You belong. Do you feel as if you 'belong' to God, and to other Christians? And are you part of a good church family? If not, ask God to lead you to the right fellowship.

Mary's story

Mary started life by being taken into care from birth. Her parents were two sixteen-year-old kids who played with sex on the way home from school, and pregnancy followed. The teenagers' parents would not take any responsibility for the situation Indeed, they virtually ostracised their children to make them pay for the trouble they had caused.

When Mary was two, she was adopted by a childless couple, but two years later they had their marriage dissolved and Mary was put back in care. At the age of four, she developed uncontrollable tantrums, was not welcome at any pre-school group and then found herself an outcast at the local primary school because of her behaviour – and, sadly, because of the way she was dressed from home. There were foster parents along the way, but only for brief spells as it seemed Mary was more trouble than she was worth. Her schooling was continually interrupted because different foster parents meant moving districts. When she went to senior school, she was bullied, ignored by most and desperately unhappy. At the age of thirteen, it was decided by the authorities that she should now stay permanently in care.

But when Mary was fifteen, one of the teachers at her school saw her plight. Mary by now had a sparse education as well as a lonely existence and unhappy way of life. Yet the teacher, who had twin daughters of a similar age, took an interest in her and invited her home for tea. Mary, very reluctant and suspicious at first, accepted the offer.

The teacher and her husband and family attended a local baptist church and, some time after their initial invitation, were able to persuade Mary to come with them on a Sunday morning. Mary had never been in a church before; her only contact with Christianity was an occasional assembly at school when the local vicar came to speak in a language she didn't understand.

Gradually, Mary came out of her shell. Though at seventeen she left school and took a job in a local supermarket, she continued attending church. She made many friends there and came to know Jesus Christ as her own personal Lord and Saviour. That began to completely change her life. She began to speak in public, talking about her new-found faith and always mentioning her gratitude to the Christian teacher and her family. She also started to attend evening classes and her education improved beyond measure. Some time later, Mary went away to college to study for Christian service. Today she is serving within a church as a youth leader, and was married at the age of twenty-seven.

She says now that she never knew what a real father was until at fifteen she was befriended by the patient teacher and her husband. Before then she would never have been able to delight in calling God 'Father' because she had only seen boys and men who were cruel, perverted and without love. Nor did 'family' mean anything to her until that point. She knows the teacher and her family took a huge risk with her. But now Mary has received true love both in a family and from God her heavenly Father.

How did Mary's teacher show her the love and acceptance of God?

It is quite possible to have what we might call a good family, a family which pulls together, but to not have a Christian faith as a basis. But when God is in the centre of family life, it is a wonderful thing.

The basis of being a good neighbour and friend

As a constable on the beat in the Metropolitan Police, my first station was St John's Wood, in north London near Lord's Cricket Ground and London Zoo. It was a varied community, from wealthy families with large houses and big gardens through to the small bedsits where many people lived alone. In between these extremes was a variety of houses and apartments. Sometimes, hidden behind the front doors, were some very needy people.

Calling one morning before breakfast to a smallish two-bedroom, semi-detached house, I was met outside the home by apparently concerned neighbours. Neither of them had seen the elderly occupant for about a week. I asked the sensible questions. How often was she seen at home and out shopping? Did she have any relative or friends nearby? Could she be on holiday? Has she been ill and might she be in hospital? I have to say, in my naivety as a young man, that I was appalled by their lack of knowledge about their respective neighbour. To all my questions I had answers such as 'She doesn't mix with us' and 'I haven't seen anyone ever call at her door apart from the postman.'

With no reply when I called through the letter box, I felt I must try to get into the house. No windows were open and the doors were locked, so I went to the rear of the house and easily pushed in the French window, which was barely secure. I asked one of the neighbours to accompany me, but neither volunteered. The dreadful odour once inside the house led me immediately to believe that the occupant had died. Sadly, I found her crumpled at the foot of the stairs. She had been quite badly injured, with blood on her face and in her hair, an arm bent at a peculiar angle and her nightwear tangled round one obviously broken leg.

At that point I was startled when the letter box opened and a letter landed noisily on the wooden floor. I opened the door and called to the postman. I questioned him about the elderly lady now dead. He said he had never seen or spoken to her ...

I was born and brought up in the village of Hooley, near Coulsdon in Surrey, where neighbourliness was commonplace. I was therefore staggered by the fact that so few knew this old lady, and even they knew so little about her, didn't' call on her and didn't try to contact her earlier in the week. She may well have lived had she had medical attention after falling down the stairs. But even in a busy London street, there was no one who cared enough to call or befriend her. Before the inquest, we traced the lady's son – a well-to-do businessman – who said that he had not heard from his mother in years. To my question about why he hadn't got in touch with her, he murmured, 'We had nothing in common, and in any case, I am far too busy to travel to London.' How desperately sad!

Is there someone you feel you should be visiting or contacting?

This incident was not as isolated as you might think. During my time on the beat in an area which is known for its opulence, with wealthy families, children in public school and elegant, expensive cars, I found there was so much loneliness on the periphery. While many enjoyed living their selfish and inward-thinking lives, others were desperate for friends and for someone to take an interest in them.

Surely it is not too much trouble for us to pick up a telephone or, better still, to call at the home of someone who is unwell or injured, or has suffered bereavement? I know of a lady in a golf club who, when she joined as a new member, wondered at some of the questions asked about missing colleagues: 'Isn't Diane ill? Is she in hospital?' 'We haven't seen Mrs Mills lately. I hope she's all right.' Yet they never took any steps to find out. Then, when the absent person returned, they simply remarked, 'Oh, we missed you!' The new member digested these and similar comments for a few weeks and then offered to visit the sick or otherwise missing members herself. The power of powerlessness?

Yet who are the powerless in these situations? Certainly not those who will help whenever or wherever there is need. The really needy are those who ignore their neighbour, their relatives and their sick colleagues. A heart that is focused on others will not be consumed with self.

Jesus said that what we do for others, we are doing for him (Matthew 25:31–46). It also says in Isaiah 58:7, 'Is it not to share your food with the hungry and to provide the poor wanderer with shelter – when you see the naked, to clothe him, and not to turn away from your own flesh and blood?' This is what pleases God. And it is true evangelism – showing God's love to other people.

Love is the key

Perhaps we should take more notice of the story of the Good Samaritan (Luke 10:25–37). Here Jesus tells us what it really means to love others – and of course, love is the key. A true family, in Christ, is the epitome of God's love, not only for Christians but also for the world. God has loved this world, with all its faults, its gross indecency, its fighting, its cruelty, its greed and its neglect of children and family – indeed, with all humanity's faults. He has loved us with an everlasting love. We may be powerless in ourselves to really love others, outside of our immediate family and close friends. It can be costly to put ourselves out for other people – especially for those we don't particularly like, or are even our enemies. But we were once God's enemies and He loved us (Romans 5:10). So we should go and do likewise, loving everyone, even enemies, as Jesus urged us to do (Matthew 5:43–48). Moreover, while we cannot do this in our own strength, that's why He gives us His Holy Spirit – so He can do His work in and through us. If you need power to love your neighbours, friends, church or even blood family, then ask God. He is more than able to supply it.

Reflection

Think of someone who is very important to you. Probably you will have had to exercise much forgiveness in your relationship with them, as the relationship is so important that you have had to learn to let go of the 'small stuff'. This is what it means to truly love someone: to serve them, to put them first and to forgive offences. Meditate on how God loves us. Perhaps read the story of the Lost Son (Luke 15:11–32).

Action

How can you love your family more today? How you can show your love to God's people, the church? And how can you reach out to the hurting? Perhaps you could offer to do some small jobs for an elderly neighbour, such as some shopping or cutting their lawn. Phone, email, text or even write a letter to a friend you know is going through a particularly tough time, or someone you haven't seen in a while. If you feel you don't 'love' as you should, confess your powerlessness to God, and ask Him to love people through you.

Prayer

Thank you, Father, that you love us and call us to be your sons and daughters. Help me to love my brothers and sisters in Christ, and to extend your love to the hurting world that does not know you. In that way, Lord, please use me to show and tell others of your wonderful love for all the world. **Amen.**

CHAPTER 9

IN SICKNESS AND IN HEALTH

As Superintendent in Greater Manchester Police at Moss Side, I was glad to be involved with all ranks and not merely be the boss. Since my early school days, I had always been involved with sport (especially rugby, athletics and cricket) so that was one way of integrating with others in the force, and I joined them in playing cricket and golf. In the operational field, I would walk the beat, either by myself or with a junior colleague, and would join in with the drug squad activity. I had insisted that the men and women in that section were the fittest not only in the station but also in the community, so they were regularly working out at the gym and I was also part of that regime.

With all this physical activity, it was a deep shock when, at home one evening after a particularly hectic day, I had a severe pain in my calf muscle. The pain was so bad that my wife called the doctor at about 10 p.m. The GP soon recognised the symptoms and diagnosed a deep vein thrombosis. He called an ambulance and within minutes I was in hospital.

After a preliminary examination by staff there, I was left alone in a side ward. I overheard an animated discussion outside the door. They were debating whether treatment should start at this late hour or in the morning. Twice I heard the comment, 'If this is what we think it is, Mr Oake may not be alive in the morning to receive any treatment.' It was a severe shock to hear that – although it was not my closest brush with death.

It took perhaps fifteen minutes before action started. There were injections and blood samples were taken. I was 'tied' to the bed to keep absolutely still. I was, of course, powerless to do anything except be treated, and in a very real and practical sense, the power of renewed life came by my submission to those who knew best.

Do you know the power of renewed spiritual life by surrendering to Jesus?

Unanswered prayer

Many illnesses can be borne with bravery, fortitude and acceptance until the condition is cured either by surgery or by other means of treatment. Nevertheless, illness is a pain! It is disrupting, uncomfortable at best and soul destroying at its worst.

Believers recognise, and may even have experienced, the healing power of Jesus. One of the names of God is Jehovah-Rapha, which means 'the LORD that heals', as God Himself proclaims in Exodus 15:26: 'I am the LORD, who heals you'. Jesus spent much of His time on earth healing the sick and casting out demons that sometimes appeared to be causing illness (as in Mark 9:17–27).

It is true therefore that God can, and does, heal. But it must be pointed out that there are no blueprints concerning illness and healing. The fact is that while many people are healed, it doesn't always happen. God has the better plan!

With this in mind, if a person is prayed for and remains sick, we must be careful not to believe it is 'their fault'. If we do that, we may begin to condemn those that do not find themselves healed, adding to the suffering of the sick person. These and other similar ideas have caused unnecessary stress for a huge number of people who are ill, in pain, uncomfortable and in despair because God is not healing them and is seemingly deaf to their cries for help.

How do you view healing?

Suffering and sin

I don't in any way want to give the wrong impression about suffering. Another misconception is that illness is caused by sin. Jesus' time on earth featured countless times when He healed people, thus showing compassion to many – to glorify His Father. In John's 9:1–3 He heals a man born blind, but before doing so, Jesus is questioned about the cause of his blindness: 'As he [Jesus] went along, he saw a man blind from birth. His disciples asked him, "Rabbi, who sinned, this man or his parents, that he was born blind?" "Neither this man nor his parents sinned," said Jesus, "but this happened so that the work of God might be displayed in his life."'

While Jesus did appear to say that illness and sin could be related (see John 5:14 and James 5:14–15), it is manifestly obvious that not all sickness is caused by our transgressions. Unfortunately there is a tendency in some towards the popular 'health and wealth' gospel, which can leave people feeling that we should all be healed, always.

Yet the timing and everything else in relation to our healing – whether it happens here on earth or once we are in heaven – is surely God's sovereign will.

Are you feeling condemned because you have prayed or had others pray for you and are not healed? Talk to Jesus about it and remember there is no condemnation in Christ (Romans 8:1).

Glory to God

As I have previously mentioned, the apostle Paul had an illness that he asked God to take away, but he came to accept that it was not God's intention to heal him. As Paul describes in 2 Corinthians 12:7–10:

> *To keep me from becoming conceited because of these surpassingly great revelations, there was given me a thorn in my flesh, a messenger of Satan, to torment me. Three times I pleaded with the Lord to take it away from me. But he said to me, 'My grace is sufficient for you, for my power is made perfect in weakness.' That is why, for Christ's sake, I delight in weaknesses, in insults, in hardships, in persecutions, in difficulties. For when I am weak, then I am strong.*

Paul was testifying here that the grace of God was a better answer to his prayer than his healing would have been from the 'thorn' in his flesh, whatever that was – speculation is that he had bad eyesight. That he goes on to 'delight in weaknesses' and declare that 'when I am weak, then I am strong' shows us a very real example of the power of powerlessness. Here God was saying,

'No, I will not heal; I can be glorified more by Paul's illness.'

Do you have a 'thorn in the flesh'? It might be the result of physical illness, injury or mental issues such as depression. Know that the grace of God is sufficient for you right here, right now. He is in it with us.

In the Old Testament, in 2 Kings 5, we meet Naaman, who was the commander of the army in his country, Aram. He was a 'great man' and 'highly regarded'. We read also that the Lord had used him to gain victory and that he was a 'valiant soldier' (v. 1). Then comes that powerful word, which, as it often does, changes the whole scenario: 'but' – 'but he [Naaman] had leprosy.'

One of God's people was a servant of Naaman's wife. The girl knew that Elisha, God's prophet in Samaria, would have the answer to this illness. Naaman willingly went to see him. However, the simple instruction that Elisha gave to the commander – 'wash yourself seven times in the Jordan, and your flesh will be restored' (v. 10) – seemed to be an insult to him, and Naaman refused to do so. Fortunately, his servants eventually persuaded him to carry out the advice which the man of God had given him. We read in 2 Kings 5:14 that Naaman washed himself in the river seven times, 'and his flesh was restored'.

Incredibly, it was through this miracle that Naaman himself became a believer. So we can see that this whole scenario brought glory to God – just as Paul's thorn did.

A Mystery

When she was young, Joni Eareckson Tada received serious neck and spinal injuries when diving into a shallow pool. She would be a quadriplegic for the rest of her life. How does one accept that at the age of seventeen? Yet Joni's example and testimony of trust in God is a challenge to all who know her or have read her books. This inspirational lady has been greatly used by Jesus. Wheelchair-bound and seemingly so limited, she began to realise that God's plan for her life had not been thwarted. She is a bright, talented and vibrant lady and is a mouth artist, vocalist and dramatic speaker – and through her witness thousands have realised their own need of a Saviour. Could Joni have reached out to so many people if God had healed her?

Stories of Jesus healing the sick fill the Gospels. Faith in Him is of paramount importance (for example, it is worth reading Luke 8:40–56). But sometimes, He chooses not to heal us. Then we must believe that God still works all things 'for the good of those who love him' (Romans 8 v 28). That in itself is a test of faith.

There is more to healing, then, than we might suppose. Healing in the Gospel of John is a sign of who Jesus is (see, for example, John 6:2). When Jesus touched Legion, who was possessed by demons, He told him, 'Return home and tell how much God has done for you' (Luke 8:39). That's a good rule to follow if we find ourselves healed. Jesus is who He says He is; His Word is trustworthy and true. He is the Son of God, our healer and deliverer. However, whether we will be healed or not healed is a mystery. Some things we just have to leave with God and say, as the poor suffering Job did, 'may the name of the LORD be praised' (Job 1:21).

Can you praise God, whatever your personal circumstances, and believe He can use you, whatever situation you find yourself in?

Responding to sickness

As trusting God during times of ill health can be such a big challenge for us, here is a summary of key points to remember.

1. While the Lord can and does heal, this is not dependent on the amount of prayer which is offered, though that prayer should, of course, be continued, so long as we recognise that the ultimate result is in God's hands – His will is to be done.
2. When we are ill, we can cry out to the Lord Jesus for His healing, but we have to accept His way whatever the outcome.
3. When someone we love is ill, we should recognise again that God can and does heal, and that there is always the possibility that He will – as long as we still pray, 'your will be done' (Matthew 6:10).
4. It is foolish to decline medical aid when trained and skilled consultants, surgeons, doctors, nurses and other staff are there to give the best care and devotion to help us. Luke, the writer of that Gospel and of Acts, was a physician. God gives those skills.
5. Whenever we are ill and often at our weakest and most vulnerable – when we are at our lowest ebb – like Paul we can experience the grace of God. We, as well as our praying friends, should be saying, 'your will be done, Lord.' It is then that we again see that there is power in powerlessness. Sickness cannot have dominion over us if we believe and trust that God is ultimately in control.

6 The same is true even if we may have been ill for a long time. We may have had copious amounts of oil on our heads for healing (as advocated in James 5:14) but it has not resulted in a change. We may have had deliverance ministry if we believe we need cleansing of demons or evil spirits. We may have confessed sins that are known to us or forgiven those who have deeply hurt us, both of which can be a cause of illness, but find ourselves still unwell. What then? Do we simply give up? No. We must continue to believe that through our struggles God understands and knows how we are formed physically, spiritually and psychologically (Psalm 139 v 14). He can heal, or He may not. Yet our task is to recognise the truth that God knows best. The apostle Paul understood this – can we?

Trust in God in action

Bob Stanley – or Cuthbert as he was affectionately known – was a wealthy architect with a practice in the City. He gave his time every Sunday afternoon, along with others, to lead the Boy Crusader class at our church, teaching and explaining the Bible. He lived with his wife Betty and two children in a lovely house which they opened to young lads for evening activities such as wood carving and engraving.

Betty, however, was overtaken by a debilitating disease – a painful, tiring illness which eventually confined her to lying on a couch or in bed. Yet when my wife and I visited her at home, despite her suffering, we were the ones who were encouraged. When she prayed, it was a prayer of gratitude to God and a longing for others to know the Lord Jesus. If we asked how she was, her replies were about how she was using the telephone to encourage others, and how she was writing – even with great difficulty – to help people in a similar plight, all the while extolling the virtues of trusting God in all situations.

There was another friend of ours on the Isle of Man who was diagnosed with aggressive bowel cancer. Following surgery, with little expectation of life ahead, Ruth Anderson began to come to terms with her illness. As a result, it was always rare to meet Ruth without a smile on her face, and that never changed. She had to attend hospital regularly as a two-day in-patient to receive extra strong chemotherapy treatment. Amazingly, though, whenever we met Ruth, she would look forward to the next treatment so that she could tell the other three patients in the four-bed suites in the hospital about her love for her Saviour, and introduce them to faith in Him. She would say to friends, 'I wonder who I'll meet next. I must start praying for them now.'

What a way to deal with illness – to be positive, never grumbling and never afraid. Ruth is still alive as I write, as vibrant a witnessing Christian as you'll ever meet, even though she now also has to cope with the death of her husband.

A habit which we English people pick up early in life is that we meet people, we inevitably ask, 'How are you?' Sometimes we hardly listen to the answer, which, of course, is quite wrong, but there are occasions when you know that if you were to ask that question, complaints would be your answer. As Jesus' disciples, we should be disciplined enough to be aware that we are witnesses in whatever situation we find ourselves and however we feel. I know constant pain is depressing and how easy it is, therefore, to always be in low spirits, but what help is that to fellow sufferers and to non-Christians? Let us be positive even through the pain of disability and to recognise the power of Christ in our apparent powerlessness!

Maybe your limitations are mental rather than physical – agoraphobia, depression, fear. These can be as much of a prison as other physical limitations. Yet in all these situations – whether we are feeling crushed in mind, spirit or body – reading the Psalms can be such a help. Then we see others who have suffered before us and yet have found God in the trouble and are assured of His love, comfort and salvation. Let us too praise God.

Sheila Jacobs writes,

> *When my dear mother was first diagnosed with dementia, sadly I couldn't cope and she was taken to live in a nursing home. I asked God, 'Why?' He showed me a picture of a piece of white paper, scribbled over and ruined by dark lines. I saw a stick-person in it and knew it was me. Another person was beside me in the picture and I knew it was Jesus. 'I'm in it with you' was all I heard but the 'Why' was answered.*

Reflection

It is hard to watch someone we love suffer through sickness. And it is hard when we ourselves are ill. Think about how you react to illness. Do you trust the doctors? It is good to do so, but they are not God. Do you pray, believing God will heal? He will certainly hear our prayers. The rest is up to Him – once we leave the outcome with Him, we are choosing to accept His will be done, whether His glory be shown in

healing or otherwise. Repenting of sin, forgiveness, even deliverance may be avenues to explore. But God is sovereign when it comes to healing.

Action

If you or someone you love is ill, be encouraged that God knows all about the situation, and He is in control. Hand this matter over to God, and know that He will heal or deliver as He chooses. Also ask Him to use the situation for His glory.

However God chooses to act, though, there is much you can do to comfort those who are unwell. Pray for those who are sick this week. Encourage them with a phone call, a text, an email or a visit. Read some of the psalms to them. Make sure no one feels condemned that they are sick. Help them to know they are not forgotten by God but are still of great value and use to Him (perhaps in leading people to the Lord, such as through writing or sharing their testimony). Bring Jesus into the situation. Also practice love! For example, give a gift to an ill person, offer to do some shopping or gardening for them, or just take the time to sit with them.

Prayer

Loving heavenly Father, thank you for our health and our bodies and our minds. Lord, right now we lift up to you those who are sick [name particular individuals]. Please touch them in your grace and mercy. We don't ask this because we are worthy, but because you are wonderful. Grant us too the wisdom to know how to pray with the sick and whether to encourage them or to just be with them For we know you ask us to visit the sick, and say that when we do so, we are visiting with you (Matthew 25:34–40). Your will be done, Lord. Teach us to trust you. **Amen.**

CHAPTER 10

WHEN DARKNESS FALLS

The teaching of Jesus in the Beatitudes (Matthew 5:1–12) gives a wonderful opening to His character and His love for humankind of all nations. Each of the promises in these verses has a specific meaning but the first two are particularly eye-catching. These state: 'Blessed are the poor in spirit, for theirs is the kingdom of heaven. Blessed are those who mourn, for they will be comforted' (vv. 3–4). Firstly, they exemplify Jesus' mission 'to preach good news to the poor' and the like (Luke 4:18–19, thus fulfilling the prophecy of Isaiah 61). Secondly, they show that Jesus has a special place for those who are low in spirit or grieving.

You will remember I emphasised that 'blessed' means much more than mere happiness. Our English language is so poor and deficient in properly translating not only the word 'blessed' but also many other words such as 'love' and 'power'. But those deeply devoted men who put together the New International Version translation of the Bible magnified the word blessed to mean the ultimate well-being and distinctive spiritual joy of those who share in the salvation of the kingdom of God. We see the same idea in Psalm 1: 'Blessed is the man ... [whose] delight is in the law of the LORD (vv. 1–2). So what Jesus promises in the first two Beatitudes is a deep experience of joy for (a) those who are poor in spirit or really downcast, and (b) those who mourn the death of those they know and love. My family has experienced exactly that, and know the peace and joy that the Lord Jesus brings, in both these instances.

It is not an accident that these Beatitudes are consecutive. In this book, we have examined those that are 'poor in spirit' already – those who are in despair, with no one to help them, but who can rely on the Lord; people, believers included, who are at their wits' end in this life, and whose only hope is in God; those who are powerless, but in turning to God are given a new power to live for His Kingdom.

Are you or any of your friends currently in this darkness? You and they can turn to God – He is only a prayer away. He invites you to give that intolerable burden to Him and rely in Him to work all things together for the good.

So what about those of us who are mourning? Most of us have had that dreadful experience of grief. We have lost grandparents, parents, brothers, sisters, children, close friends, colleagues, neighbours and so on. Life suddenly seems empty, especially when death is premature through illness, accident or murder. We are sad and understandably weeping – don't be ashamed of that. We feel alone and unable to face other people even though they may be sympathetic. But we can triumph over sadness.

Remember this: Jesus himself was sad and tearful when He heard of the death of His friend Lazarus. John 11 tells us that 'he was deeply moved in spirit and troubled' (v. 33) and that 'Jesus wept' (v. 35). In that sadness He was able to be with Lazarus' sisters Mary and Martha. He came alongside and listened to them; He comforted them. Jesus hasn't changed!

Many can testify about Jesus and the deep peace and strength that He gives in bereavement. At such times we are at life's lowest ebb, yet it is when we are in this place of complete powerlessness that we may experience God's power.

If you are mourning, ask God to especially comfort you by His Spirit as you read this chapter.

As I recounted in chapter two, our detective son, Steve, was killed during an arrest. His assailant was convicted of murder and later convicted of terrorist offences. It was all a numbing shock to our daughter-in-law and her three children – our grandchildren, as well as to Steve's two sisters and, of course, to my wife, Chris, and me. We had learnt a strong lesson some time before Steve died, which I've also mentioned earlier, namely that we should never ask God in tragedy, 'Why? Why have you done this, God?' Instead we should say to our Father in heaven, 'What now, Lord?' In other words, 'Lord, this happened. It is so painful, but what do you want us to do right now and in the future without Steve?' Nevertheless, of course we were deeply shocked and deeply saddened, and the media, like an army, was adding the pressure of us being in the full glare of the public eye.

We hit rock bottom; we were powerless. But in that very weak state, we all experienced the power of God lifting us up to triumph in His grace. At Steve's funeral service, which was a celebration of both him and all that we have through Jesus, we were able to say to the world, 'There is triumph out of tragedy!' In Manchester Cathedral that cold day were a huge number of friends, colleagues and others whom we didn't even know, including the then Prime Minister, Tony Blair, and his wife. Having spoken to many of them, we know that they were deeply moved at the positive note throughout the worship, Bible readings and addresses. In welcoming the 1,000 strong congregation, plus the hundreds outside the building to whom the service was relayed, I was able to say, 'We never say "goodbye" to a fellow Christian who has died; we quietly say, "au revoir; see you later." That is one of the blessings of which Jesus spoke. Steve himself knew that for him to die was gain, as he entered into eternal life (Philippians 1:21).

Have you lost a loved one who was a Christian? Be comforted that they are with the Lord and that you will see them again.

Peace

Peace can be found even in the direst of circumstances. Paul wrote in his letter to the Philippians:

> *Rejoice in the Lord always. I will say it again: Rejoice! Let your gentleness be evident to all. The Lord is near. Do not be anxious about anything, but in everything, by prayer and petition, with thanksgiving, present your requests to God. And the peace of God, which transcends all understanding, will guard your hearts and your minds in Christ Jesus (vv. 4–7).*

Peace can be found when our prayers are voiced to God. By trustfully praying to Him, we unburden our heart, divest our anxieties and release the grip on our grief. Instead we can gain the peace of God – an inexplicable, divine calmness of spirit. This peace supersedes our ability to understand our circumstances and is a guard on our heart, through Jesus. Paul writes specifically in Romans 8:26: 'the

Spirit helps us in our weakness'. We don't have to go it alone.

Do you feel as if you are 'going it alone'?

Reaching out to others in your grief

In the midst of our grief over Steve, we were reminded of the Lord Jesus on the cross who, in His agony, was thinking of others: His mother, whom he placed in the care of His beloved friend, John (John 19:26–27); the repentant thief, whom He declared would that day 'be with me in paradise' (Luke 23:43); His enemies, both religious and pagan, about whom He said, 'Father, forgive them, for they do not know what they are doing' (Luke 23:34).

So this began a new pathway for us: to think of others through Steve's death. Others I know have had similar experiences: a Salvation Army captain, whose son was also killed by a terrorist; Anne and Brian, whose pilot son, Allan, was killed in Afghanistan; Hil and Will, who lost their son, Tom, while he was coaching in Las Vegas, before Hil then lost her husband through cancer. As those who mourn, we are conscious of God's presence, for He gives us comfort, deep peace and a new outlook. Following this, our attitude should be the same as that of Christ Jesus, looking to the needs of others. We should say, 'Others, Lord, yes, others. This is my motto too: others, Lord, yes others, that I may live like you.' Here we see again that in such a situation there is power when we feel so helpless and powerlessness. Out of calamity comes opportunity; we can choose whether to stay with the calamity or to look for the opportunity.

Don't forget that 'Jesus Christ is the same yesterday and today and for ever (Hebrews 13:5). He also says, 'Come to me, all you who are weary and burdened' – such as those who are grieving, who are inconsolable, who are weeping with sorrow – 'and I will give you rest' – I will comfort you, you who are so low and poor in spirit (Matthew 11:28). Be healed by Jesus, but then be used by Jesus to take Him with you into similar situations. That is why I ask if I might pray with the bereaved if I go to visit them. I want grieving people to know that there is light at the end of the tunnel, even though it may not be seen at present; once round that bend, light can be seen and we will get out of that dark place.

We always need to be ready to share with others about Jesus – especially with people who face death as they have a terminal illness, or have been seriously injured, or have had a sudden heart attack, all of which makes them recognise that their time on earth is very limited. I realise how difficult it is sometimes to make conversation in such circumstances – some don't want to talk or might reluctantly listen anyway. Nevertheless, speak carefully, and be a good listener to them too.

I am wary of deathbed conversions, but I well remember those Wyn Baker told me about. When she was in hospital with inoperable cancer, Chris and I went to visit her to bring cheer to her and her husband, Len. Yet each time we arrived, Wyn would greet us with a broad smile, speak of all that she had learnt in her quiet devotional time (even though this was in a busy ward) and then relate how this patient and that patient had asked her about her vibrant faith, and how some had learnt to receive Christ into their life and trust Him.

Death is not necessarily the end; it can be a beginning. And ultimately, as we will know if we read of the believer's glorious future in the last pages of Revelation, we have much to look forward to once our earthly journey is over.

Dealing with suicide

Perhaps the worst scenario for a police officer is to be called to a home, a field, a wood or somewhere else to find a body with gunshot wounds, or an empty drug bottle next to a corpse or a hanging. Sometimes the death has been discovered by someone else. At other times the police have been called in because a friend or relative has sensed that something isn't right or because a person hasn't been seen for some time.

My colleagues and I could never get used to such situations, especially because initially we had to deal with it dispassionately as a crime scene. Occasionally what we were called to had been a set-up following a cold-blooded murder or an accidental death which, through guilt, someone had tried to fudge, so the full circumstances had to be investigated.

However, where it was a genuine suicide, I read some heart-rending notes as to why people had taken their own lives. It appears that the intention to take one's own life is rarely a spur-of-the-moment decision.

At one dreadful scene, I discovered the crumpled body of a lady in the basement area of a block of flats in Paddington, London. She had evidently jumped from a fourth-storey window but had left a note on her dining-room table which simply stated, 'I can't stand living anymore.' She was a very lonely lady with few friends and a distant family, and she had discovered that she was seriously ill. Another note, following a hanging, which was duplicated to the man's wife, children and work colleagues, expressed deep remorse about his actions and the feeling that no one could ever forgive him. I pity the relatives and close friends in such circumstances. They are the ones left to bear the grief, the shame, the accusations. The suicide note will often give away secrets that cause guilt which cannot be repaired. Even worse is the suicide without any idea of 'why'.

If you have been affected by suicide, have you been able to talk to someone you trust, such as a counsellor or minister?

There is nothing so final as taking one's own life. Where there's life, there's hope. Even with a terminal illness, modern science has made dying naturally, albeit with an incurable disease, possible without pain and with much comfort. When a relationship breaks up, even with that awful feeling of being let down, it is not the end of the world. But leaving this world and going into the next is a serious business.

You will sometimes see at busy road junctions that yellow criss-crosses have been painted across the intersection. In order to prevent vehicles clogging up the adjoining roads, these warn you to enter a box junction only if your exit road is clear. The allegory is a stark challenge: you want to make sure that before you are brought into the box (your coffin), your exit is clear, that is you are absolutely assured of eternal life in the kingdom of heaven!

This should be the warning if you are tempted by, or are driven to think about, committing suicide, as well as at any time when death could be imminent. Of course, though, it is better to be right with God when in good health since, as we have already discussed, death can happen all too suddenly. We all need to be properly prepared that our 'exit is clear'. For the Christian, going through the dark doors of death holds no fear as Jesus promises all believers eternal life with God (John 11:25) in heaven, where a place has already been prepared for us (John 14:1–3). I cannot shy away from mentioning the other place, which is the destination for all those who don't believe in Christ. It is surely awful to contemplate hell and damnation and their judgment to come, but the Bible tells us clearly that this is the case (Hebrews 9:27).

With this in mind, if you are feeling the powerlessness of being in the depths during this life, do not contemplate ending your life – it is not the answer. Rather invite Christ into your situation – then you will experience power. When Jesus takes over, He can give peace to your mind and soul, and bring a negative situation to one of positive thinking. If we love Him, our Lord has His hand on us – whereas with suicide a person is actually taking their life into their hands. God holds the key to our life, if we let Him unlock it. Even at our lowest ebb, putting our trust in Him can mean a new experience of abundant life.

Are you feeling desperate? Turn to Christ. He knows you, He understands, He will not condemn and He will never let you down. He has the power to heal, deliver and set you free.

On Vauxhall Bridge

Once two of my constables at Rochester Row Police Station were in the Area Car. A call went to Alpha 1: 'Vauxhall Bridge: man in distress on parapet. Approach with caution from the north.' This was 3.20 a.m. on a winter's night. As an Inspector, I was the Duty Officer and, having heard the message, kept a watching brief from a distance – I was near enough to give assistance but far away enough to not interfere with my two constables. I also called the Information Room to have the Thames Division attend the scene when I saw that my colleagues were talking with a man who was on the river side of the bridge and likely to fall in the fast-flowing water.

I watched my colleagues evidently pleading with this man – who was in his thirties, well dressed and not under the influence of drink. While watching, I directed other colleagues to seal the bridge from north and south, and called for an ambulance, which drew up alongside me. After nearly three-quarters of an hour, I radioed my men and asked if they needed any help. They simply asked if maybe I could come and assist them as they were not 'getting anywhere, boss'.

I walked slowly up the slight slope of the bridge. There was an eerie silence, since there was no traffic. As I got nearer to my colleagues, I could hear a stilted conversation with the hysterical man and began to recognise what was being said. The man was threatening to jump. He was speaking in a high-pitched voice, pleading to be let go of by my colleague, who was bravely holding on his arm. They were both leaning out over the murky water, on the river side of the balustrade.

As I arrived, slowly, I heard one of the constables say, 'This is my boss – he will be able to help you. Why not listen to him?' I introduced myself and coaxed the man back to the pavement, where we both sat down and I listened. My two colleagues backed away. The man told me his story, which was one of a difficult and broken marriage; of a job which he felt was too hard for him and stressed him out; of such dreadful headaches, with it taking too long to diagnose the problem; and of feeling that he had no friends and that there was nothing left for him in this world. I asked him why he hadn't jumped before the police arrived and his reply showed the nature of his problem. He said, 'I wanted to end it all but I hadn't the guts to do it.' He feared the unknown.

After another half an hour, I persuaded him to get some treatment. He was taken to Westminster Hospital, where I kept in touch with him by visiting him and, in time, I shared my testimony about faith in Jesus. He was diagnosed with a brain tumour – the cause of his headaches – which, after other treatment by drugs, was ultimately dealt with by surgery. As our friendship developed, he warmed to the gospel and eventually sought forgiveness and received Christ into his life. He now had a quite different perspective on life and began to face his problems. His marriage mended. He was treated well by his boss while on sick leave, then some months following his return to work, he took another more suitable job. He found friends near his home, most of them at the church which he was now attending.

The power of Christ met this man's desperate need; he now has hope and can face what was to him an unknown future on both sides of the grave. Thank God for His power to change lives. We are never as powerless as when we are facing death. Yet we can thank God that Jesus has conquered death for us, so we can have eternal life (John 10:28 and 11:25; 1 Corinthians 15:55).

Reflection

If you are grieving, and if the person who died was a believer, begin to look forward to the fact that one day you will see them again. If you are mourning for one who did not know the Lord, trust God with the detail. If you are facing the death of a loved one, remember Jesus never leaves us; He is 'in it with us'. He has said you are 'blessed' when you mourn, for you can know the very real comfort of the Holy Spirit.

Action

Meditate on Revelation chapters 21 and 22. Whether you are facing death, or are in the process of grieving, it is good to remind yourself (and loved ones) that, for the Christian, the only hell we will ever know is on this earth. We will all face death one day, and the more people we can take to heaven with us, the better! Is there anyone you can witness to at this time?

Prayer

Holy God, please fill me with your gentle and gracious Spirit. Give me the power to cope at this difficult time. I can't do it on my own, but I know that you can. I fully rely on the One who said He is the resurrection and the life. Praise your Name, Jesus. **Amen.**

CHAPTER 11

LIFE IS NOT TROUBLE FREE

I guess that this book and all the different situations we have covered is addressed by the apostle Paul in seven reassuring words: 'the Spirit helps us in our weakness' (Romans 8:26). Paul is talking here about prayer and that sometimes we really don't know what to pray for but that the Holy Spirit understands our deepest needs and intercedes for us with our heavenly Father. How many times do we hear the name of God uttered by people either in distress or when in a happy mood? His name frequently trips off the tongue, often of unbelievers, but only as an exclamation when there is no intention of invoking our Father in heaven.

Yet this book can be summarised by the fact that God knows all about our struggles – He not only knows our situation but He also knows the solution. He longs for people to involve Him in them. However, and very sadly, if we who acknowledge openly that we walk with God by trusting the Lord Jesus don't then 'walk the talk', there is nothing in us to advertise that He is the answer to our every need.

True Christianity

Why should we shy away from true Christianity? And why are we so shy about our faith? A powerless life of weak and watered-down belief can be transformed by the Holy Spirit into powerful and attractive lives for the Saviour who gave His all for us.

Do we want wishy-washy Christianity, with its mere outward expression of putting on our best clothes and turning up at the local church on a Sunday? No; walking with Jesus should mean spending time with God each day and speaking with Him as we walk, as we work and as we meet with friends and neighbours. Some may shun the addict, the alcoholic, the homeless, the wastrel and the beggar. Wonderfully, our heavenly Father rejects no one! Anyone who truly seeks Him will find Him, and will find in Him everything that is needed. This is love unmatched by anyone, and love without condemnation for all who trust in Jesus' death on their behalf. He is the Almighty Authority, our God and Father. He has a Mighty Motive, which is a bottomless love through which He sent His Son to die for our sins, as seen in 1 John 4:9. He has given the Greatest Gift – not only our forgiveness but also the fact that through Jesus we are declared innocent rather than guilty (Romans 3:23 24). He has the Widest Welcome: 'everyone who calls on the name of the Lord will be saved' (Acts 2:21). He gives us the Priceless Possession, which is everlasting life, as opposed to the Awful Alternative of perishing for eternity (John 3:36).

Do you feel rejected? Know and believe that God does not reject you, whatever you have done, if you turn back to Him.

Surely in life most of us would be completely satisfied if we had lives of peace – if we were at peace with the world and with each other. I guess that would be the wish of a huge number of people. Yet living in the twenty-first century, there is anything but peace. Nor can peace be found by living in isolation or by opting out of society, because that not only cuts people off from the warmth of friendship and hospitality but also can leave one with a very low opinion of oneself and open a door of depression. However, Jesus promises us peace; He is called the 'Prince of Peace', and we are called to follow Him.

Nevertheless, true Christianity does not mean that life will always be trouble-free. Jesus said we must live a life of self-denial – the way of the cross (Luke 9:23 and 14:27). To do that really is walking the talk. Following Christ may bring division (Luke 12:49–53), which does not make for easy reading. There is a cost to consider when we think about following Jesus (Luke 14:25–35). So we may have peace with God, and we are called to live at peace with others, but we may not find Christian living easy. God must come first; that means everything and everyone else must come second, or at least that we must be prepared to give them up, as we have seen in the story of the rich young ruler (Luke 18:18–30).

Have you counted the cost of following Jesus?

Christianity is a serious business. But if we feel we cannot live for Christ, we can know that He will give us the power to do so.

The alternative

We have already thought about death. At death we are at our weakest, for the body has shut down and there is nothing we can do about it. But if we are prepared for eternity at any time in our life, it doesn't matter whether we die suddenly or at the end of a prolonged illness. It is our relationship with God the Father through His Son, the Lord Jesus Christ, which determines our future after we die. The Bible is very explicit about eternity, explaining heaven and hell and who goes where.

Someone once said to me:

> *Robin, just supposing you are wrong about all this and I am right? I have enjoyed a good life and I believe that when I die, I simply don't exist any more. I haven't had to spoil my Sundays by going to church; I haven't had to put up with the ridicule you have had by being a Christian. I have worked hard and played hard; I have travelled far and wide; I have a lovely wife and children who have done well for themselves. What more do I need? I have no regrets. We only live once and I have enjoyed my life.*

On one point there, my colleague was right – we only live once in this life on earth. But there is life beyond death and what happens after our earthly life is determined by our response to the gospel.

I am sure my reply wasn't as lucid as it might have been, since this person threw the question at me without warning. However, I said something like this:

> *I understand what you are saying, but you have presumed to think that I have not had a happy and fulfilled life. The presence of God is with me. My daily prayers and Bible reading plus walking in His way are very satisfying. I have the assurance that death is not the end but the beginning of eternity. Despite the tragedy Chris and I had of losing our son*

through the knife of a terrorist, with God's help we have come through it, positively. God has sustained us all as a family.

Just supposing I am right, then, and you are wrong? When you have died and meet your Maker, He will ask what you have done with His Son who loved you and died for you. It will be rather too late to say, 'Nothing,' or, 'Well, I knew Robin, please let me into heaven.'

Remember that time I met a lady on my beat who I knew slightly and who I helped with her shopping. An opening came to speak of my faith, but she cut me short by saying, 'Young man, you don't need to worry about me. My nephew is the Bishop of Norwich!' Yet, sadly for her, being a Christian and having eternal life is not something which can be inherited or passed on from others. Believing in Jesus and receiving Him in one's life has to be a personal decision and invitation.

Have you made that personal decision to believe in Jesus, or are you trusting in someone or something (even good works) to get you into heaven?

Ultimate power through death

Just as we have to be prepared for death, however it comes, Jesus spent His years on earth tasked with that difficult but necessary preparation for His death. He knew it would mean excruciating pain. But He faced it, and through His willing sacrifice, He has opened the door to humanity to have a relationship with God. As He said in John 10:10: 'I have come that [you] may have life, and have it to the full.' Jesus came to offer us new life, and an eternal life.

Most of us celebrate Christmas, as far as possible, with our family and friends. The celebrations usually involve bright lights, festive cards and messages of love as we share our gifts. The sad thing about this is that the central figure of Christmas – Christ Himself, who should be the focal point of our celebrations – is all too often omitted, forgotten, seen as irrelevant or not even known about.

To me an eternity with God is far too long and too wonderful a future to waste. Heaven is something to which I can look forward, though my anticipation is spoiled by the fact that so many of my friends have failed to recognise that Jesus Christ is Lord.

God offers us a place in heaven for eternity, in a new heaven and new earth where there will be no more pain or suffering. 'He will wipe every tear' from our eyes. Indeed, the old order of things will have passed away (Revelation 21:1–4). Whether we die or are whisked away when Christ comes a second time (1 Thessalonians 4:16 17), we have a glorious future. If we have committed ourselves to Jesus, we may stumble and fail in our Christian walk, but He promises us the power of His Spirit so we might live in victory – the victory He has bought for us on the cross when He triumphed over sin and Satan, and which gains us eternal life. Thus, ultimately, when at death we are at the point of complete powerlessness and can do nothing to save ourselves, we find ourselves, in Him, to be victors – eternally. There is no real powerlessness then, only the inestimable power of God as we find ourselves in eternity with Him.

Will you be there?

Reflection

Think about what you have read in this book. What are the points that have stuck with you? If you have made any notes, review then. If you have reflected on or completed any activities, think about how God has spoken to you through them.

Action

If God has been speaking to you, write down anything you think He may have said about you, your life and your circumstances. Has He challenged you to follow Him first? To take your commitment to Him more seriously? To let go of things you cannot change, and trust Him to do His work in and through you – and to love others in and through you, too? Is there something He is asking you to do, specifically? Perhaps to get baptised, go into the ministry, serve Him in a different way, visit someone who is sick or get involved in evangelism, sharing the gospel with a person who desperately needs to know Jesus? Maybe He is asking you to forgive someone, or ask for forgiveness. Perhaps He is just asking you to make more time for Him – to regularly read your Bible, pray and sit in the quiet enjoying His presence while He restores you. 'Do whatever he tells you' (John 2:5) and trust Him for His power in your powerlessness!

Prayer

Jesus, I know I am weak. I cannot live the Christian life in my own power. But you give me the power to live for you in whatever life you choose for me. I surrender to you now. Thank you for your salvation, your Spirit, your love. Use me today. Let me do the Father's will in your strength, not mine. And may your name be glorified in my life now and for always. **Amen.**

CHAPTER 12

THIS IS THE CRUNCH

I learned at school never to start a sentence with 'and', yet with this final chapter I do so deliberately following all that you have read in the pages before. Likewise you should never start a sentence with 'but', and yet ...

AND now, what about us who love the Lord Jesus and not only worship Him but try to serve Him? Most of us enjoy Christian fellowship with fellow believers. We enjoy attending church services and activities. We might even be a leader of a young people's group or a small Bible study group, or may sing in the church choir or ring church bells – a whole spectrum of service.

BUT what about evangelism? What about speaking to others about our faith – our family; our next-door neighbours; the community in which we live; our colleagues at work; those with whom we play sport or with whom we socialise; those we meet at the doctor's surgery, on the bus or train, while in hospital and speaking to nursing staff, medics and other patients?

If you are like me, you don't find evangelism easy. I am, perhaps, too reticent even when asked about my faith. Many of us would rather keep silent. We feel powerless to do anything. We don't want to put people off, embarrass them or be critical of their way of life and so on. And yet they should know that Jesus died for them, Jesus loves them and He would welcome them to be His disciples.

It may be helpful for you to know that although I have been a police officer in every rank and am now involved with The Order of St John and the Royal British Legion, I am always very nervous when I have to speak, either formally or in council. At the National Police College, Bramshill, I along with all other potential senior officers was trained hard for my future role and given special training in formal speaking. I was also trained in my early years as a Christian to lead church services and preach, and even took on the role of pastor for a number of years at a church in the Isle of Man. Yet, I am always nervous when I stand to lead or speak, at men's breakfasts, dinners, church services and other occasions, despite years of doing so ...

As I have already mentioned, years ago there was a time when I was with two colleagues from the Christian Police Association and we were serving as a team to speak at a chapel in south-east London. As we met together with the church secretary before the meeting, one of our number prayed, 'Lord, give us nerves so that we rely on you and not on ourselves!' I butted in, saying aloud, 'He has answered that prayer long before you asked!'

Having confessed all this, I know I have an obligation to speak in my secular roles and even more so in the Lord's service. I thank God that although I am nearly shaking when I stand up, He gives me utterance and the strength – the power out of my powerlessness – to go on.

I am an avid reader of United Christian Broadcasters 'Word for Today' since it is always very apt. Recently, I read from their daily bulletin the following: 'in Christ we who are many form one body, and each member belongs to all the others' (Romans 12:5). That reminds me of the words of an American veteran who was part of the D-Day invasion (the massive military force sent from France to England to overthrow the forces of Nazism). He said D-Day was the most frightening experience of his life. 'In fact,' he said, 'I don't think some of us would have been able to do what we did if it weren't for a visit we got just before we crossed the English Channel.' That visit was from Winston Churchill. He rode up in a Jeep, got out and mingled with the troops. 'He shook hands with us and even hugged some of us,' the veteran recalled. 'He spoke of his own wartime experience and identified with our emotions. Then he stood up in his Jeep and gave a five-minute speech. He spoke the whole item with tears in his eyes.'

Here's what Churchill said:

> *Gentlemen, I know you are afraid. I remember being afraid when I was a soldier. I had the privilege of defending my country ... through dark days when we didn't know whether we would accomplish what we had been given to do. But this is your moment. We are counting on you to rise to the occasion and achieve everything you have set out to do. The fate of the free world rests on your shoulders. May this be your finest hour.*

The American veteran finished by saying, 'Needless to say, our group of frightened soldiers turned into a band of men who were ready to take on anybody.' Togetherness is a powerful thing when you put it into practice!

Likewise what encouragement we Christians have in the 'battles' we face and as we foray into the world to be reliable and powerful disciples for the Lord Jesus. As Christians we are not unique since we all have the obligation to witness, and all of us recognise the difficulties that there are in speaking to others about our Saviour. Moreover, we form one body and each member belongs to all the others, so we should share our fears and share how we have coped with the problems of witnessing, and we should be praying for one another as well as encouraging each other.

I am reminded of the apostle Paul's words to the Corinthian Church: 'When I came to you, brothers, I did not come with eloquence or superior wisdom as I proclaimed to you the testimony about God ... My message and my preaching were not with wise and persuasive words but with a demonstration of the Spirit's power, so that your faith might not rest on men's wisdom, but on God's power (1 Corinthians 2:1–5, my italics). When we witness in whatever way – of course, it may not be speaking at all but through giving a helping hand, listening to a tale of woe or visiting a patient in hospital or in a hospice – we do so in the strength which God supplies through His Son. What is more, it is in our daily quiet time of Bible reading and prayer that we are equipped for the day ahead, empowered by the Holy Spirit and alert to the opportunities we are given.

Churchill's way of meeting the troops and addressing them before the battle is so pertinent to us in a spiritual sense. The Lord speaks to us, emboldens us with His strength and keeps us watchful for the openings to share His love. Furthermore, Churchill's words had extra resonance because he had been to war himself and was wounded in South Africa while fighting for his country in the Second Boer War. Our driving force is that Jesus Himself faced the perils of this world, before going to the cruel cross with all that shame and crippling pain. More than that, He rose from the grave and is alive today, encouraging us in the battle.

We Christians should also have the comfort of praying for and supporting one another. Our mutual goal should be that we daily 'set apart Christ as Lord' in our lives and will 'always be prepared to give an answer to everyone who asks [us] to give the reason for the hope that [we] have' (1 Peter 3:15).

I end by underlining and emphasising that we are not trying to get people to follow us but, as Paul states, are playing our part that others may find faith. We are not resting on our wisdom, but on God's power. Nevertheless, how wonderful it would be to echo these other words of Paul's: 'Pray ... that whenever I open my mouth, words may be given me so that I will fearlessly make known ... the gospel' (Ephesians 6:19).

I wonder if I could finish with what I hope is an appropriate analogy. I was assisting others to remove the pews from our local church and, in a crack, found two old pennies, one dated 1915 with King George V's head thereon and the other dated 1946 with the head of King George VI's head thereon. At both those dates the pennies had the same value but, having been lost in our church, their value had since decreased almost 100 fold. Being in church had certainly not added to their value. Is that a picture of any of us who are church attenders on a regular basis but rarely if ever witness to anyone outside the building? We almost decrease our value to the gospel for others, despite being children of the King of Kings, because we have not taken the gospel out into the world and proclaimed it.

Reflection

The following verse contains three challenges and three promises I commend it to you. 'Be strong and be brave. Don't be afraid ... because the LORD your God is with you. He will not fail you or leave you' (Deuteronomy 31:6, taken from the ERV Bible).

Action

This is practical Christianity and underlines the fact that our faith in Jesus Christ is not a simple matter of belief and going to church. Instead it is a matter of not only putting into daily practice our trust in Him but also demonstrating to all who know us that our faith is working.

Prayer

Lord, you know me better than I know myself. I want to serve you in any way you choose and I need your strength to do that. So that my life will point to you, help me to see the opportunities to speak and live for you, and, Lord, please give me the courage and strength to be a strong witness. In my powerlessness, use me, Lord, to reveal your power. I pray in the name of Jesus. **Amen.**